AUTISM AND THE POLICE

of related interest

Caught in the Web of the Criminal Justice System
Autism, Developmental Disabilities, and Sex Offenses
Edited by Lawrence A. Dubin, J.D. and Emily Horowitz, PhD
Foreword by Alan Gershel, J.D.
Afterword by Tony Attwood
ISBN 978 1 78592 713 3
eISBN 978 1 78450 298 0

An Employer's Guide to Managing
Professionals on the Autism Spectrum
Marcia Scheiner (Integrate Autism Employment
Advisors) with Joan Bogden
Illustrated by Meron Philo
ISBN 978 1 78592 745 4
eISBN 978 1 78450 513 4

The Autism Spectrum, Sexuality and the Law
What Every Parent and Professional Needs to Know
Tony Attwood, Isabelle Hénault and Nick Dubin
ISBN 978 1 84905 919 0
eISBN 978 0 85700 679 0

AUTISM AND THE POLICE

Practical Advice for Officers and Other First Responders

Andrew Buchan

Jessica Kingsley Publishers
London and Philadelphia

First published in 2020
by Jessica Kingsley Publishers
73 Collier Street
London N1 9BE, UK
and
400 Market Street, Suite 400
Philadelphia, PA 19106, USA

www.jkp.com

Library of Congress Cataloging in Publication Data
A CIP catalog record for this book is available from the Library of Congress

British Library Cataloguing in Publication Data
A CIP catalogue record for this book is available from the British Library

ISBN 978 1 78775 284 9
eISBN 978 1 78775 285 6

Printed and bound in Great Britain

Contents

Introduction

The police carrier stopped suddenly outside the rear entrance of the custody block and a large officer jumped out. Red faced, he grunted, 'He's been kicking off all the way here, sarg. Bloody fought like a cornered dog, vile he is.'

The carrier shook violently, side to side, as if there was a caged animal trapped within. Screams of profanity, muffled by the thick cage in the rear, drifted out.

'I would stand back, sarg, we'll get him out.' The officer put his large hand out to emphasise the point whilst being joined by the driver, an equally huge bloke.

I stood back slightly to allow the doors to swing open, revealing the offender cuffed to the rear, bouncing around, swearing and spitting at the two officers.

They stood back to avoid to the barrage, 'See, told you, sarg, never flaming right this one,' said the first officer.

I looked at the small figure, instantly recognising him as one of my regulars. I relaxed, knowing exactly how to deal with him. Trying to cut through the tremendous noise and to the surprise of all present I barked, "Kevin! Behave!'

The figure immediately stopped, looked towards me and raised his eyebrows. After a few seconds, a comprehension enveloped him and he visibly slumped. Speaking in a hoarse voice, he said, 'Sorry boss, it's them, they've treated me like a bloody animal, look, bloody cuffs are cutting me hands off!'

He turned to show me the handcuffs, which were obviously biting into his flesh.

I had no worries dealing with this individual; turning to the driver I said, 'Get the doors open, I'll bring him out.'

'But he'll kick off, sarg,' he replied, shaking his head.

'Not with me he won't, will you Kev?' I looked directly at the detained figure.

'No boss, never, not with you,' he replied softly.

The cage was opened and I assisted the young man down the steps and adjusted his handcuffs immediately to a more comfortable position. 'Now, we are going into custody and you are going to behave yourself aren't you, Kevin?'

'Yes boss, is me mate on?' he asked excitedly, referring to one of my custody detention officers CDOs.

'Yes she is,' I replied.

'Sweet, she's ace she is…and you are, boss, dead fair you are, not like these arseholes,' he said flicking his head towards the arresting officers.

'Kevin, behave,' I said sharply.

'Soz boss,' he replied, dropping his gaze.

Kevin was booked in without any further incident and eventually placed in a cell with his usual cup of hot chocolate, after he had been allowed to fold his own outer clothing taken routinely from him as part of the booking-in procedure.

'How do you do it, sarg?' asked one of the perplexed officers after Kevin was led away by his favourite CDO.

I then explained to yet another untrained officer that Kevin was autistic and I had been dealing with him for several years, and in that time I had developed a strategy, tailored to him, as I had done with anyone who I suspected was autistic.

In the ten years I spent in custody, I realised that there was a lack of understanding from bobbies about people who are vulnerable and in particular autistic. The working strategies I designed for all of these people who were presented to me came from having to work closely with detainees for up to 13 hours a day. This means you see how people are when they enter custody and how they leave. In those hours in between you are sometimes the only person they see and have plenty of time to discover how they tick.

I booked in hundreds of people like Kevin, both male and female. With each one I learned as quickly as I could to find a way to reduce their anxiety, which is the main trigger for uneven behaviour. I controlled the environment they entered and I was able to change it to suit their needs as best I could within my working parameters.

My starting position was to give everyone who walked through the door the respect they deserved and *earned*; it wasn't just given willy-nilly. There was a code that I expected to be followed, which kept everyone safe and by it they knew their detention would be the same every time they came in.

I didn't 'pander' to them, but I tried to accommodate everybody's needs as best I could and it nearly always paid off. Sometimes it didn't; there are some people who flatly refuse to engage, even with added intervention but, in the main, it had a positive outcome and in some cases even a success story.

I was a front-line police officer for 27 years and a sergeant for over ten years. I was lucky enough to work on lots of different sections and experienced many of the darker parts of police work, the things that leave a mark on you. These all added to an ability to thrive in the final segment of my career, the custody block. This is not a place for everyone and I regularly saw colleagues put in a transfer to leave as soon as possible.

I found it an invaluable way to help the constant stream of vulnerable people who were unfortunately incarcerated. I saw that by working with them, rather than against, significant changes in offending behaviour could be made. I learned an awful lot from being 'locked up' with them and used that knowledge every day to make a difference for all the 'Kevins' of this world.

The other tool I had in my 'box' was my diagnosis. I am autistic.

I found I could spot another neurodiverse person – an umbrella term used to describe people who have autism, dyspraxia, dyslexia or attention deficit hyperactivity disorder (ADHD) to name a few, from now on abbreviated to ND – being brought into my custody block, far more quickly than any of those around me. I had a unique insight into their feelings...as an autistic person.

I am not claiming I had an in-built diagnostic machine; I didn't need one. When I saw someone who acted like me, it made me immediately think, 'Are they autistic?'

It was those comments from all of the officers who had not received *any* training in autism that lead me to develop many protocols and systems within my force during my final few years.

This book is the culmination of all the work I did on a daily basis as a police officer coupled with the extensive work I carried out within the autism and learning disability arena right across Great Britain.

It has been specifically designed to give you, the officer, a unique insight into the world of autism, because it has been written by one of you, a police officer with autism. All of my experience has been distilled into relevant, honest advice to genuinely help you on a daily basis.

I will show you how to avoid getting disciplined or, even worse, dismissed for doing something that so easily can be avoided.

Read the book. Learn from it. This could be the only time you will have the opportunity to have a 'get out of jail free' card, when it comes to carting someone into custody. Think of how many times you have dreaded having to take 'one' in, for an offence which is bound to be later on, No Further Action. I can prevent that, given the chance.

You don't need to read the book from cover to cover in one go (although I do recommend it) as each section contains all you need to know about that specific subject. I have done all of the hard work for you. There is no studying, no exam to pass, just simple information contained within these pages. By following the Golden Rules which I have set out for you in an easy-read format in Chapter 2, you can make someone else's life better and possibly even your own too.

This book contains strategies, examples and clear debriefs to show you what to do and more importantly what *not* to do. I am going to give you a toolkit to help you spot, manage and assist people with autism.

You may now be thinking, 'So what? How often am I likely to come into contact with someone with autism?'

This is a fair question and I will answer it:

There are many different estimations for the number of autistic people in the world. The figures quoted vary massively, so for the sake of argument let us take the following as a starting point:

One autistic person in every 100 people.

Consider that, for every 100 people you encounter, at least one will be autistic. So on a football match duty you have a crowd of 20,000, so mathematically 200 of them will be autistic. Right, you now have a group of 200 of them coming down the street towards you, all wearing scarves and waving flags. Do you know how to deal with them?

I do, and I will teach you.

Also, from research that has been done, there is a significantly higher chance of an autistic person becoming embroiled in the criminal justice system (CJS) and I will show you how.

Stick with the book. There are a few parts that may seem 'textbook' speak but it is all relevant to you and your job. Reading it all will give an understanding of how the autistic mind works (mine at the very least). I can give you that edge that other books can't. I designed systems that circumnavigated all of the problems I personally encountered. The use of these will save you time and effort and keep you out of the custody block far more than you otherwise would be; better still it could keep you off the dreaded 'POL 1' or constant watch duty.

The advice is also not limited to people with autism. It will work for anyone and in particular vulnerable people. The start of the knowledge is simple:

Treat all autistic people with respect and as human beings.

Does this seem ridiculous? It isn't. As a person with autism, I have heard and seen discrimination and, even worse, a dismissive attitude. People ignore or overlook autistic people, treating them as if invisible and having little value in society. This could not be more wrong.

A common misconception is that autistic people do not think, feel or love.

They do.

Sometimes they will feel and think a lot more than you.

Do not assume anything with autism. Ask. Talk and listen to the person – you may find you are surprised by their answers.

I will show you just how far all of this can go by giving you practical demonstrations of how autism presents and what may be behind that behaviour, because there usually is something rather obvious you have missed. However, once trained by this book, I hope you will never miss it again.

Background

This book will set out the process for someone, even without autism training, to be able to identify an autistic person, deal with them effectively and sensitively, if absolutely necessary detain them and then assist them in their journey through the CJS and beyond.

This book has been primarily produced to assist the police service in dealing more effectively and fairly with *all* neurodiverse people, but particularly those who are autistic. Although written with the CJS in mind, the information contained can be used by anyone to help any vulnerable person. The advice is equally pertinent to all of the other emergency services and in particular their first responders. These are the people who are usually first on the scene and have initial contact with a vulnerable person. If trained in autism they will have a significantly increased ability to deal with the person in the correct manner.

In this book, I have used the term 'officer' to identify the person dealing with any of the scenarios. However, this term can pertain to anyone dealing in the whole criminal justice process.

A police officer is usually assumed to be front line and in uniform. Although it is for them that the majority of the information in this book has been designed, the modern police family now has many members, all with valuable contributions to the CJS.

This book can be used in the training of the special constabulary, police community support officers, Criminal Investigation Department (CID) and specialist interviewers, as although their training covers vulnerable people, few courses have an extensive segment on autism.

Having worked with all departments at every stage of the CJS, I quickly realised that many stages make up a chain, which needs each of the individual links to be as strong as the last. With this in mind, the information you read starts from when the call about the autistic person arrives at headquarters (HQ) and the call taker, to a despatcher (if different), to the officer being sent (you), to the custody sergeant (if the arrest is unavoidable) to the interviewing officer (you again), through to the court and support teams there.

This chain is used in the scenarios and each link is shown how those people can improve in the way they deal with autism, because they all *can* improve. I do not consider myself omnipotent, so neither should you. No matter how much training you receive, there is always more you can learn. Autism is a complex subject and even I am discovering things about me, every day.

The lack of understanding of autism within the emergency services is causing many situations where an autistic person is ultimately arrested unnecessarily. With the correct quality instruction, the rates of detention can be reduced. By showing how it can feel to be autistic when dealt with by a person of authority, I will explain how, with the right approach and interventions, arrest and detention can be avoided.

The examples contained in the book are taken from real situations I personally encountered but the people, places and situations have been changed to maintain the anonymity of those involved. They have been carefully selected to highlight areas that commonly arise for officers and give a step-by-step guide to deal with the autistic person in order to achieve the best outcome.

I have designed the book knowing that front line officers are extremely stretched and have time constraints on them as well as a supervisory officer or a control room badgering them to be free as soon as possible to attend the next job. I am also acutely aware that the police are usually the first people to attend an incident and in the main have received little or no training in how to deal with autism, neurodiversity or mental health issues.

This guide contains numerous tips on saving time, blushes and even lives in the most extreme case. Used correctly, it could be the saving grace you need when dealing with any vulnerable, and in particular autistic, person.

The advice contained within its pages is designed for an officer who, faced with something that looks unusual, will have these words jump into their mind:

STOP. THINK. Is this autism?

And by thinking these five words it is just possible that they may save that officer's career.

The following report is extremely important and impacts upon your daily duties without you even knowing it:

'The Bradley Report', Lord Bradley's review of people with mental health problems or learning disabilities in the criminal justice system in April 2009.[1]

The report by Lord Bradley was a comprehensive review of people with mental health problems or learning disabilities in the criminal justice system. It encompassed and impacted on all people with neurodiversity who were vulnerable coming into contact with any parts of the CJS.

Why is it important to you now?

From this comprehensive report commissioned by the government, the police were shown to have the most important role when dealing with vulnerable people in our society. As a service the police could identify, intervene and divert them away

---

1   www.basw.co.uk/system/files/resources/basw_120004-10_0.pdf

from custody in the first stage and use the court process only as a last resort.

Highlighted in the *Early intervention, arrest and prosecution* section, the police stage was then the least developed in the offender pathway. Although this report is now over 10 years old, the systems outlined in the report are still relevant today.

His findings are fair and quite reasonable. It is how these are interpreted that has been a bone of contention. Out of his main suggestions only one was acted upon by the police service with any vigour:

The revamp of neighbourhood policing was suggested, trying to move away from traditional 'Dixon of Dock Green' style foot patrol to a more cohesive and interactive strategy involving the communities they serve. This all-too-tangible concept was introduced right across the UK. As a first line of contact with the autistic community, it could have been so easily combined with the other suggestion, which was not introduced with nearly as much determination.

A clear recommendation was:

Community support officers and police officers should link with local mental health services to develop joint training packages for mental health awareness and learning disability issues.

This can also be taken to mean autism. I personally received very little input in these two areas and certainly had no training or guidance of substance around autism.

Not much has been developed to assist officers identify and deal with the people most vulnerable in our society and Lord Bradley's findings still stand. Officer training in autism is negligible across the whole of the UK police forces. There are pockets of good work being done but as a whole the quality of instruction of officers in this vital area needs to be improved.

An excellent way of introducing autism awareness to officers would be a training package delivered personally by quality agencies that would enable them to more effectively engage with the vulnerable sections of society they meet on a daily basis.

By 'quality training' I mean: training done preferably by autistic people, but if not, by people who have the full backing of the autistic community, have a deep understanding of how autism affects someone on a daily basis and vitally by a person with a sound knowledge of the CJS.

The training must be delivered sensitively and with meaning, so those attending can clearly see how their use of intervention techniques will stop the person with autism suffering. Ultimately the information must be relevant to the officer and how they can relate it to their daily duties. Once learned the techniques can then go on to assist the officer when all else around them is impeding their role.

What is clear from the report is the number of unnecessary arrests of mentally ill or neurodiverse people there were year on year. With the correct intervention by the emergency services this could be dramatically reduced; simply by applying the rules in this book, an officer can avoid having to detain an autistic person. One of the intentions of this book is to prevent as many of these unnecessary arrests as possible and you can make this happen.

Chapter 1

A Guide to Autism

What is autism?

I will explain what autism is, why it is important that you understand all of the different aspects of it and how it will impact on your role as an officer.

Search for a definition of autism and you will more often than not come across something like this:

> Autism is a lifelong condition, present from early childhood, characterised by great difficulty in communicating and forming relationships with other people and in using language and abstract concepts with repetitive behaviour, narrow obsessional interests, resistance to change, motor-coordination difficulties and unusual sensitivity to the environment.

This stereotypical explanation is sadly lacking in depth for what is an incredibly complex neurodiversity. As an autistic person, I can state that autism is the way in which I experience the world around me, how every part of it impacts on every second in every hour of my day.

It can be from the small worries trying to prevent you from getting out of bed in the morning to deciding if you can physically face the world outside your own home. It can make me extremely anxious but can also bring a great deal of pleasure when I see the beautiful symmetry contained in the natural world around me.

I choose to classify myself as autistic rather than a person with autism because that's what I prefer. However I leave it entirely up to the individual to decide if and what they wish to call themselves when it comes to autism. I was 'given' a diagnosis of Asperger's but I feel that it has an aspect of superiority attached and with it comes a connotation that you are high functioning and therefore more able than other autistic people. For an autistic person, it can be the environment around them that causes the disabling elements in life and has nothing to do with intellectual ability. Throughout the book in using the term autism or autistic I include Asperger's or Aspergic and neurodiverse.

In this book you will see I switch from using the term autistic to 'person with autism'. I have deliberately chosen to use both, either or neither where appropriate as I feel comfortable with either of these terms. Please be assured that no disrespect is intended to anyone. For you as an officer, as a rule of thumb ask the autistic person you are dealing with what term they wish to use throughout your involvement with them.

Terms used in the autism world

These are some of the most used phrases and acronyms concerning autism you may encounter. It is important that you listen carefully for someone mentioning any of them as the person you are dealing with may prefer to use an alternative word to autism.

ASD – autism spectrum disorder.

ASC – autism spectrum condition. Alternative to ASD and sometimes seen as less controversial.

The spectrum – an umbrella term often used to describe someone who is autistic, further linked with the phrases low functioning or high functioning.

Asperger Syndrome (AS) – also termed as Asperger's or Aspie. Derived from the name of the doctor, Hans Asperger who worked on autism in the 1940s.

Neurodiversity (ND) – an umbrella term created to refer to people who are autistic, dyspraxic, dyslexic, have AD(H)D or all of the other acronyms contained in this book.

Neurotypical (NT) – the majority of people in the world who think and act in a way which is considered usual, 'normal' and conforming to the confines of society.

SSB – self-stimulatory behaviour, better known as stimming or self-stimulation.

Meltdown(s) – a phrase used a lot in the autism world to describe the behaviour of an autistic person when they are overwhelmed by their environment. You may see this as outburst or as an extreme shutdown. Either is equally distressing to the autistic person.

These are a few more words used in and around the autism community. As with the ones above I have only laid out brief explanations but urge you to seek further information from local or national support organisations as they are the people who know best. As with any other situation mentioned in this book, treat everyone with respect and care.

ADD – attention deficit disorder.

ADHD – attention deficit hyperactivity disorder.

CD – conduct disorder.

Dyscalculia – a specific learning difficulty affecting numbers.

Dyslexia – a specific learning difficulty affecting reading.

Dyspraxia (DCD) – developmental coordination disorder. A lifelong condition affecting fine and/or gross motor coordination.

Echolalia – the repetition of words, phrases or noises made by an autistic person.

Learning disability – term used to describe a reduced intellectual ability and difficulty with everyday activities that is lifelong.

OCD – obsessive-compulsive disorder.

ODD – oppositional defiant disorder.

PDA – pathological demand avoidance.

Tourette's syndrome – a neurological condition that causes involuntary sounds and movements, referred to as 'tics'.

What autism is not

There are many explanations for what autism is and very few for what autism is not. It is important that myths and conjecture are dispelled in order that you have a greater understanding:

- It is not a disease and needs no cure.

- It is not something to be embarrassed about.

- Autism is not just another word for 'naughty boys syndrome'.

- It isn't used just to obtain a blue badge and free parking pass.

- Autism is not a 'label' or 'a series of acronyms invented by pharmaceutical manufacturers as a way to sell its drugs', as I was once told on an autism awareness course.

- It is not something only found in childhood and you do not grow out of it.

- Autism is not a mental illness.

- It is not a walking list of stereotypes.

- It is not just boys but also includes girls. It is not just men but women too.

- It is not full of 'Rain Man' types.

- Autistic people are *not* monsters who will attack you upon sight.

- No one ever has the right to abuse a person with autism, condemning them as a 'second class' citizen.

People who live with autism every day, those with it and those who care for or support them, work hard to secure their rights as defined by law to live a similar life to you. A lot of families rely on the diagnosis they were given to enable the person with autism to access what they are legally entitled to receive. The complex diagnoses many people receive gives them a clarity with which to understand how they have felt all of their lives and can be a way to explain their very challenging life.

With the correct support around an autistic person, they can achieve incredible feats, which can be a rewarding and positive experience for everyone involved. All they need is respect and understanding, something which all of you take for granted as part of your daily lives.

In this first example below, I set out a simple scenario that you as an officer could encounter every day. Imagine you have been called to a suspicious person at a railway station and how you may deal with them.

It is designed to show how devastating something simple, such as a change in circumstance, can be to a person with autism. Understanding how an autistic person can 'freeze' to the spot or fail to react to your speech is the first step in dealing with them effectively.

EXAMPLE 1

Eddie is 20 years old. He is 6 feet 2 inches tall, as thin as a bean pole and has a mop of thick black hair. He loves German heavy metal and listens to it on his MP3 player whenever he can. His coat has a large hood that he places up to shield him from the world around him. Both hands are rammed into the bottom of the pockets, where they will stay until he boards the train.

Standing on the platform at his local train station he eagerly awaits the 9.15 into the city to attend college. Another of Eddie's passions is rail transport. He has always liked it, the way the massive engines draw the carriages and the smell of the stations add to the pleasant experience he receives from being around them.

What Eddie doesn't like as much is inside the carriages. He really doesn't want to share them with anyone else but knows he has to when travelling. The seats feel very rough, which is a strange mix of good and bad. The smells from the people around him are not so nice; they sometimes hit his nose and it stings sharply. He tries to block it out the best he can and concentrate on the trains.

His acute hearing suddenly tunes into the 'fizz' of the tannoy before the announcer speaks. Even over his music he can hear the man speak; unfortunately for him he can hear the people too.

'Will passengers waiting to board the 9.15 to the city please relocate to platform 3B on the other side of the station. Due to a points change the train will now be arriving on platform 3B... I repeat...'

People charge off towards the staircase behind Eddie. They jostle and jockey for a better position, carrying luggage and coffee cups. Nothing seems to bother them; they swarm like ants to their mound.

Eddie stands perfectly still. He is standing in his favourite place, the one he uses every day. He likes this spot; it makes him feel comfortable and fits his body exactly. He can see the people running down the stairs to get to the edge of the other platform first, smug they have beaten the others to it. Eddie remains perfectly still.

He can see the train now pulling in. The announcer reports its arrival and yet he remains perfectly still. The train fills up with the snarling animals from the platform, the doors close and it begins to pull away. Eddie remains perfectly still watching it pull away.

After all around him calms, he blinks, sighs and slowly turns around. Tomorrow it might not happen, he might get on his train as he usually does, but today he will go home and lie on his bed in the dark. The fear inside him screams, yet on the outside he is silent. This is how his autism feels. He hates having to give in to it but he has no choice: his autism controls...him.

DEBRIEF

Something this simple, just changing location from one part of a train station to another, may seem inconsequential to a neurotypical person, but to a person with autism it may be enough to withdraw and not board the train they so long to be on. This illustrates how even the smallest day-to-day occurrences can be a challenge, stressful and draining for those who are autistic.

You should be now able to see how light, sound and smell all impact heavily on Eddie. He has acute senses and heightened reactions to the environment around him.

So, you have been sent to deal with Eddie. You approach him and receive no reply. Is he ignoring you? Could he be hearing impaired? Or is he guilty of something? These are all thoughts that may pass through your mind.

The first thought from now on should always be, 'are they autistic?' From that base you can move on to any of the others in this book, but this will be a safe place to start, every time.

I am now going to examine autism in more detail, as there is so much more going on underneath the surface. How the person reacts to you will nearly always be determined by how they are feeling. So let's start with the first section, the senses.

The senses

Everyone is aware of the five senses: touch, hearing, taste, smell and sight. You use them all day, every day. Something as simple as turning on a kettle and watching it boil whilst getting a cup, the jar of coffee, milk and sugar is second nature to you. When you see the steam rise and hear the button click off you know what is happening, there are no other interferences to concern you. Reaching out for the handle, your senses are expecting the weight of the water, heat from the liquid and where the cup is to pour into. It is all carried out seamlessly and effortlessly.

For a neurodiverse person those hardwired pathways to the brain can be broken or missing, which causes something so mundane to be a nightmare to carry out. Where the kettle is suddenly becomes all-focusing and new techniques may have to be brought in each and every time, just to make a cup of tea. In a crowded or noisy environment imagine your senses being like an old-fashioned graphic equalizer. The row of buttons is used to filter sounds up and down. Whereas you can tone down a ticking clock or noisy fan, a neurodiverse person may not be able to. You can set that equalizer how you wish; the sounds are amplified to zone in on something quiet or faded to decrease them. The opposite can be true for neurodiverse people. They may have no control over the buttons all being pushed up to maximum or down to minimum or even turned off completely, all without warning. These differences may seem quite trivial but having little control over your senses can be quite overwhelming.

When introducing the senses it may seem pointless to you, a busy officer, that you should be interested in how an autistic person is feeling. You can't see inside, so what's it got to do with identifying someone with autism?

It is exactly because you cannot see what is going on that you will be at a disadvantage. The swirling senses hidden beneath the surface of an autistic person are the very things which drive every movement. Once you understand how they impact on your interaction with them, then you will be better equipped to handle the autistic person sensitively.

When an autistic person walks into a new situation they can be bombarded by dozens of experiences an NT person automatically filters out. Most of the time the autistic person has very little or no control over how they react to it. With careful preparation, an autistic person can train themselves to deal with the disgusting smell from an air-freshener in a toilet they have visited before, but being hit by an overwhelming set of ceiling lights in a meeting room they have to sit in, is something they can do nothing about.

Although the senses have traditionally been classed as the basic five, studies have expanded the definitions adding several more. The last three deal with how a person experiences the space around them, the balance mechanism of their body and how their internal organs feed back information to the brain.

How all of the senses work, particularly the last three, is vital for an officer in understanding how a person with autism is reacting to them. Their mood, speech, movements or lack thereof may have a lot to do with how these senses are working overtime to feed data back into their brain.

Never assume you know how the person with autism is feeling; ask them, and if no information is forthcoming then use the information contained in this book to form a possible answer until local data is available. Try to discover and understand what is impacting on them and then what you can do to help them deal with it.

By understanding the senses, you will be able to see how draining the world can be for an autistic person. They often describe social interaction as a necessary evil to obtain what they need from the NT world. Having 'fitted in' and mixed, they retreat to the safety of their homes to 'recharge' their social batteries, which can take as long as a week to complete. This is for something they are prepared to do; imagine how it would feel to do something they don't want to do or have no control over, such as interacting with you.

If you have the power to control the environment an autistic person is in, then use that power to adjust it to suit them. Giving them this small courtesy can be the first step in showing them they can trust you. Something as simple as closing the blinds or opening or closing a window or door during a meeting can be such a relief to a person with autism. It may then enable them to be calm enough to focus on the situation at hand. Imagine someone is sitting next to you and prodding your arm constantly during a briefing. Would you be able to concentrate? How long would it be before you became annoyed? How much of the information would you absorb? This is how it can feel to be autistic.

When a bright light is above you, a clacking fan is on in the room or someone's perfume drifts up your nose, it can be so overpowering that you switch off everything else and fixate on that one thing alone. Remember, an autistic person will have absolutely no control over it at all and will be unable to filter any of these things out.

So when dealing with an autistic person, in any environment, think about how it is for them or better still ask them, as they are the best source of information. If they are too shy or unable, ask their carer, as they will know them better than anyone else. Whatever the cause of the distress, however minor it may seem to you, it will be all-consuming to them. Just stop and think, be accommodating; it will serve you well.

Sight

- The first thing an autistic person will probably encounter is your uniform. It doesn't matter if it is black, green, yellow, blue or orange; it is the colour that could be offensive or even attractive to them. Be aware of this fact. The same can be said about civilian clothing – the colour of a shirt, blouse or scarf can present as exactly the same. Be careful to note any reaction that you receive.

• The colour, shape or pattern of the clothing can 'hurt' the person's eyes. This is a really tricky concept to explain to NT people. The nearest approximation is the sting of eye strain after hours staring at a computer screen. That sharp, sudden pain that tells you that a break is needed comes close to this sensation. Imagine that pain hitting you unexpectedly when you see a colour or pattern; it is that explosive to the sufferer.

• It can also be said that certain shapes or patterns are enticing. The lesser criss-cross pattern of a reflective jacket, hidden behind the main colour, can be really soothing on the eye in the same way as it may be painful. This could distract the person, so if you can remove it from sight, it could aid communication.

• Bright lights are always mentioned by everyone when discussing autism. This is not because there is little else: it is really important. As a doctor's eye torch seems to find the back of your skull with its intensity, so it is with room, car or street lighting for autistic people. It feels as if your eyes are being burned out or your head is being crushed, similar to a severe headache (which it can go on to cause). Do not ignore a plea from the person regarding this, deal with it.

• A really important piece of information for you is this: your uniform may *not* be recognised by the person with autism. Just because you know you are a police officer, they may not. Do not expect them to react with respect or compliance because you want them to. Tell them who you are and ensure they understand before you demand anything from them.

Sound

- Similar to light, sound impacts just as heavily on the senses. The pitch of the sound is equally important as the level of noise and the length of time it is heard. Everyone has encountered the unwanted fire alarm. That screaming noise that seems to drill into your head. This level of disruption to thought can be exactly the same as your mobile ringtone; not everyone likes the theme tune from *The Bill*. If you really don't need to have it on then switch it off. The sudden ping of a text or the buzzing of the vibration mode is very distracting but can be disturbing to an autistic person.

- The wail of emergency sirens is especially painful, as anyone who has stood on a busy high street will attest. This seemingly mundane tool that officers use daily can sometimes be disregarded. You become immune to the changes in pitch as your brain filters the familiar frequencies out. I couldn't. I had to switch it off or change to another one, as it became painful for me, even after seven years on the traffic section.

- The source of siren sound is in close proximity to a passenger and whilst trapped in an emergency vehicle, sound waves bounce around the inside of the vehicle, distorting it further. If the siren doesn't need to be on, then switch it off. It is a simple thing to do and eliminates another small amount of stress for the autistic person.

- When interviewing/obtaining a statement from a person with autism think about the noises around them. In an interview room is there a fan on? This sometimes 'whirring' drone can be like a dentist's drill in the brain. If the situation dictates, switch it off. The recording machine you are going to use may have a noise to indicate it is starting or working; explain this to them. Do not assume they know anything; tell them everything.

- Unexpected noises can be the worst. Something that may make you look up could make them jump. This jarring may not leave their body for seconds, minutes or even hours. It can feel like an electric shock – real pain. I cannot labour the point enough. If something happens and the autistic person is seen to react (even in the eyes) then ask them if they are okay and give them time to calm or process the event.

- If you know in advance that there are certain noises in the environment you are entering or are going to be in, then tell them this too. Explain slowly and carefully what they are and why. Reassure them that their appropriate adult (AA) is there with them and you will do everything you can to make the event as comfortable as possible.

- When dealing with an autistic person in an outside environment, consider what the noises around you are likely to be doing to them. If they are in a crowded street, try taking them into a quiet shop doorway or just into the edge of an alleyway. However, be careful about taking them too far away from the street they were in. The anxiety of the new area may cause a shutdown in communication. Explain why you are doing it and *ask* them, is it okay? Do not assume it will be better for them because it may be for you or you think it will be.

Smell

- How this sense impacts on an autistic person can be quite confusing for neurotypical people to comprehend. A smell you cannot detect may make the autistic person retch. Autism can seem to come with a senses button turned up to 11. The slightest whiff of a scent can be enough to completely disorientate the person. It can be overpowering and they may not be able to circumnavigate it, as it will be there constantly. Once again, imagine something that you hate the smell of, something really vile, enough to make your stomach heave. Place that reaction at the front of your mind. Is it making you sweat? It can do that. You will have fought the urge to vomit at some point in your life, possibly in your career; I know I did at the very first postmortem I attended. That smell has stayed with me for 30 years and I think always will. For autistic people, many smells can be like this. Work with them and listen to what they are saying to you.

- Do not dismiss this information as fantasy or being oversensitive; it will be genuine, as you will see their obvious reaction. If they or their carer have the courage to tell you, believe it and change location if you can. I am not asking you to pander to a suspect, however you are not going to obtain a true account if they are constantly heaving through the process. Ask the AA if there is anything that will alleviate it. Maybe a cup of coffee could mask it or is it your coffee that is doing it? Remove whatever the offending item is (if possible) and reassess.

- It could be they react badly to you. Do not take this personally. It might just be the smell of your cologne or perfume, even the wash powder you use. This simple fact can be a barrier to them in dealing with you or the area they are in. Don't be shy, ask them: 'Is it me? Can you smell something on me you don't like?' Autistic people can be direct, so give them the same level playing field. It could work to your advantage. If it is you, figure out a way of removing the smell. Will a wash with soap on your neck where you sprayed a perfume solve the problem? Be flexible and be patient.

Touch

- From speaking to many autistic people the one thing they report they do not like is to be touched, particularly without prior warning and permission. The rule of thumb is:

    > If at any point it can be avoided then **do not touch** a person with autism.

- Being touched by someone, especially when they are not aware of it coming, can be shocking – literally. The feel can be like an electric shock, a painful nip or a burning squeeze to their flesh.

- Think back to your time in the gym doing self-defence. The first time you were placed in a strangle hold or pinned face down for a cuffing drill, it wasn't pleasant was it? All you wanted to do was break free and stand away from the perpetrator, didn't you? This is how it will feel for an autistic person. That sense of panic, not knowing if you are going to be released, goes some way to highlight the power you have in your hands.

- Or you may have been in that situation when you have had to deal with someone you really did not want to touch. It could be their dirty clothing, blood-stained garments or that they were soaked to the skin. When you first put your (probably gloved) hands on them, that initial revulsion or panic illustrates how it is for an autistic person to be touched. They may even feel unclean from being touched by you.

    STOP. THINK.

    'Would I want to be grabbed like this?'

- If at any point it is no, then back off and reassess *before* you do it. Remember how it feels for you and afford them the same respect.

- Even a 'shepherding motion' with your arm across their back may cause a flinch. Watch them closely; if they do not try to run from you or escape, then perhaps it is the touch that has caused it. If you honestly feel you need to take hold of them, then tell them you are going to do it. To many officers this will feel completely counterintuitive. You are trained not to divulge any techniques you are going to use in an arrest situation – why would you? This is a different playing field; the autistic person will possibly have no idea what you are there for and will be offering very little threat. As with your training, go in stages until they offer violence, then stay in a heightened state of awareness; be alert and responsive but *not* hands on.

- Do you really need to handcuff them? Could you sit by them and watch them instead? Are they offering violence or resisting or is it because you 'always' cuff them? Assess the situation; if there is any chance of not cuffing them, then don't. The cuffs, as we all know from training, are vile. They feel sharp and uncomfortable. They are designed to do this to discourage offenders from being non-compliant. STOP. THINK. Do I really need to use these? If the answer is no, then do not do it just because it makes *you* feel better.

- Ask the person with autism if you can place a hand on them, or if it is a cuffing method for transportation, tell them: explain it is the law and it is for their safety as well as yours.

- Whenever there is a possibility of relieving any situation that is impacting on the autistic person, such as shifting the cuffs, sitting further away in the car, standing back in custody, then do it. If you do not have to be in direct contact with them, don't.

- An equally confusing concept for NT people to grasp is the need to touch something. This need to touch somehting can include compulsion or obsessions which I will cover in more depth later. However for now, think of it as if you enter your favourite shop, the one you love going in most. Maybe it is for a new jumper, towels or shoes. Imagine everything is behind glass. You cannot touch any of it. You can see it and even smell it but cannot touch it. How frustrated would you be? After long enough you would be so incensed you would do anything to touch it. This is how it may feel on a daily basis for a person with autism navigating the world around them.

- For an autistic person the filter switch not to do this can be turned off or not even exist. They will simply find it too hard to resist and do it. This type of behaviour can be just as overt as the urge to retreat. It could be that an autistic person is detained at a large art gallery where they have leant over the barrier and stroked the display, causing damage to it. It may be this compulsion that brings them into contact with you.

- It could be that when dealing with the autistic person, they are touching an object near to them or stroking something on them like a button whilst you talk to them. This will not be designed to annoy or distract you but may be the only way they can cope with the stress of the situation and making them do it in front of you.

- Remember the advice above and find out what has caused the act or made them do something in front of you and deal with it sensitively.

Taste

- This should only really fall into the custody category unless it forms part of an investigation. In the unlikely event that the person with autism has used their taste sense at the time – perhaps they were drinking a hot chocolate as the offender pushed them – listen to how they talk about it. The act of drinking the liquid and the sensation it was giving may be important. It can also help to follow a thought stream. Using a cognitive approach by placing them back at the scene: that feeling, taste or warmth of the drink could hold all of the clues to the incident around them. The same can be used for anything placed in the mouth. Offences against the person could involve taste; using this technique could be invaluable in these circumstances.

- However a note of caution at this point: placing an autistic person in a cognitive state can be just as painful to them as when the offence/incident happened. They will relive it as it has just happened; being instantly back in that place and at that time could distress them too much to give an account. Work with them and use a sensitive approach tailored to them. Consider support post-interview.

- Whilst in custody the person with autism (the detainee) has the option to eat and drink. Although the food has improved (in some areas anyway) it is still quite unpalatable compared to their usual meals at home. Remember this. They may not be able to eat because of the smells in custody; the cells are rather unpleasant places. If they are hungry they may not know it due to a lack of sensory feedback or being too scared to ask.

- If they refuse food/drink ask them again a few minutes later. Enquire as to why they have refused: 'Are you okay to eat hotpot?'... 'No'... 'Why?'... 'I don't like it'... 'Have you had it before?'... 'No'... 'Would like to try some?'... 'Er yes please'.

- It might be that they are unfamiliar with everything on your menu. A lot of autistic people stick to the same food every day, as eating the same food comforts them. They may eat bland or 'beige' food because the colour of some food is distasteful to them. Ask them, talk to them, try to understand they are stressed and their senses are on alert, they are scared and just want to go home.

- The same can be said for drinks. It may be the cup; styrofoam is an awful substance for most people. Confirm that the cup is clean. A lot of autistic people do not like to touch something that they have not seen cleaned in front of them. This may overlap with obsessive-compulsive disorder, but treat their fears as purely that: a genuine fear. Try to allay them as sensitively as you can.

You have probably never heard of the next three senses – proprioception, the vestibular system and interoception – but they have a huge impact on how a person functions. The way in which they affect an autistic person will explain why they do something or move in a particular way.

The way in which you might see these manifest whilst on duty is if the person you are dealing with stumbles, trips, appears generally 'clumsy', invades your personal space, ignores your demands or seems overly nervous. Autistic people can feel anxious about situations they cannot predict or control and seem reluctant to change.

They may react unexpectedly because all of these senses are on alert, which in turn may bring them into contact with you. After the initial assumption that they are intoxicated has passed through your mind, consider autism.

I will return you to the train station from earlier. There you will remember all of the NT passengers going about their business without a problem. They swerve and dodge up and down stairs, carrying luggage and coffee effortlessly, arriving at a new destination ready for the next task. For a neurodiverse person all of the required movements may seem insurmountable, as they did with Eddie. He was not able to change platforms due to an invasion on all of his senses.

Whatever you see will be as a direct result of anxiety and out of their control.

The next time you happen to see anyone in a public space who seems lost, scared or shut down:

STOP. THINK. Is this person autistic?

Anxiety in autism

This is such a huge area of autism that I felt obliged to dedicate an entire section to it. Each and every part of autism is overshadowed by anxiety, which manifests in myriad ways. For some it may simply be a faint worry about the unknown; in others it may dominate their entire life. There are certain things that can be done to ease it; however, do not expect to banish it entirely.

A general definition of anxiety is:

A feeling of worry, nervousness, or unease about something with an uncertain outcome

or

Strong desire or concern to do something or for something to happen.

Anxiety affects both the body and mind. The psychological symptoms are hidden and anxiety may only ever be recognised when the physical symptoms are visible. From the sufferer's perspective, the cycle in which they find themselves may not even be discernible to them. The physical will often overlap or blend with the psychological, blurring which is which.

The lists below have been taken from the NHS website.[1] Note that they are not exhaustive or the symptoms mutually exclusive.

The psychological symptoms of anxiety:

- restlessness
- a sense of dread
- feeling constantly 'on edge'
- difficulty concentrating
- irritability.

The physical symptoms include:

- dizziness
- tiredness
- a noticeably strong, fast or irregular heartbeat (palpitations)
- muscle aches and tension
- trembling or shaking
- dry mouth
- excessive sweating
- shortness of breath
- stomach ache
- feeling sick
- headache
- pins and needles
- difficulty falling or staying asleep (insomnia).

---

1   https://www.nhs.uk/conditions/generalised-anxiety-disorder/symptoms

What anxiety actually is, from the inside, is a feeling of horror, a deep fizzing in your stomach that can radiate throughout your entire body as a freezing or burning. It goes hand in hand with fear. It may be fear of the unknown, of the known, of certainty just as much as uncertainty. It can be anything. About anything. Nothing is too trivial for anxiety and certainly nothing is too big. It eats away at you, destroying anything in its path. It comes in levels and they can be built on as each new obstacle is met until you are at breaking point. Along with anger, it can dominate all of your thoughts and block thought patterns, preventing you from doing anything.

This is a good point to revisit the term 'meltdown'. It is a word I loathe, basically due to the extremely negative connotation it has attached to it. I have times when I am overwhelmed by the environment I am in. It may have started days previously and built up to a meeting I am attending or a hospital appointment. It matters not what the trigger is, it is the feeling inside I am experiencing that will dominate my entire thoughts until the situation has ended. The nearest comparison for an NT person to grasp may be a panic attack. At that time in that space I have little control over my emotions and have to shove them deep down to hide them and 'assimilate' into the NT world in which I am forced to participate.

I have thought long and hard about a replacement for 'meltdown' and have found nothing I agree with. 'Environmental impact factors' is too wordy but it is exactly these which dictate how I feel. 'Emotional disruption' is another but seems too clinical, so until I create the exact one, being 'overwhelmed' by the situation will have to do.

Returning to the pressures of anxiety I will use a simple scale of 1 to 10 to show how it feels on the inside. There are many scales, including butterfly to face charts. Some have their place, others frankly don't. If we stick to a simple ten-point scale I will illustrate how anxiety creeps in and then controls the mind and body.

As can be seen in this thermometer of anxiety, it goes in stages. Do not assume that when dealing with a person with autism that they will be standing in front of you at level 1. It would be far more sensible to assume that simply because you are there it will be creeping up and already at 3 or 4. Also the autistic person's anxiety and anger gauges can shoot from 1 to 10 in a matter of seconds.

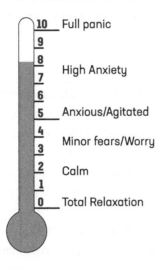

Many autistic people have issues in both of these areas. Their gauge can shoot up to 10 without conscious recognition. They sometimes describe it as a 'fuse board'. Imagine a row of house fuses, sitting under your stairs. These are the trigger sensors in your brain.

Unlike NTs who have the ability to use other cognitive processes to acknowledge rising anxiety and stem or suppress it when they feel it is getting out of control, an autistic person may not be able. It is not a conscious decision to become anxious or angry; it may have occurred entirely without them knowing.

If they meet a situation they are deeply unhappy with, such as crowded places or shops packed with people, then their coping fuse may just pop out and that circuit is now defunct. Once this has happened, they will either shut down and not be able to function properly or feel angry and have to leave immediately.

Be careful when dealing with any person with autism; consider how they are feeling all the way through, even though this will be difficult for you to consider in an active or conflict situation. However, not all situations are like that, as you will see later on.

The next example shows how anxiety can be a slow-burning issue that results in you coming into contact with the person.

EXAMPLE 2

Susan is an autistic adult. She has an appointment with her social worker to discuss how they access the new sports club opening in town specifically for people with additional needs. This is a good thing and Susan likes participating in sports.

The problems started when Susan was told (by someone she trusts) that the club was being opened. At that point anxiety set in.

When does it open? What is the club? Where is it? Will I like it? Will they like me? What sports will they do? Will the lad from the centre who bullies me be there? The list goes on ad infinitum.

Susan, who was at level 1, is now pushing level 2. For the neurotypical mind the concept of something so benign triggering anxiety may seem ludicrous. To a person with autism this is a very real concern and only the start.

We return to Susan, several days away from meeting her social worker (someone she also trusts and likes). Seeing them is not a big problem but 'going' to see them is. So rather than her anxiety dropping down it continues at 2. Many other things are still impacting on her life, nothing of note but the daily problems of life such as what to eat, how her family are and the health of the cat, to name but a few.

In the background the appointment is preying on her mind. Susan sees it every day on the calendar, where her carer has placed it to remind her. Sometimes she does need reminding of things as if they are not important they tend to slip her mind; but this is, and Susan won't forget.

The day before the appointment, Susan gets up after a bad night's sleep as it is now really worrying her. Just the night alone has pushed the anxiety up to a level 3. The day has started badly; she is tired and even more worried.

Susan has now realised she will have to go on the bus to the day centre to meet the social worker. What bus? Will it arrive? Will it smell bad? Where will I get off? Will I be late? Susan likes buses and travelling on them, but this is not sufficient to drive down the anxiety and it creeps up to a level 4.

Susan's carer tries to explain it will all be okay and helps her calm down with all of the valid techniques they have been taught. Unfortunately, the carer mentioned in passing that they saw roadworks at the corner of the street that morning. Susan feels roadworks are bad and her anxiety pushes to level 5.

As you can see, the halfway point on the scale has been reached over just a few anxious moments. Susan is receiving good support from the people around her and everything has been put in place to help; however there is nothing that can stop this onward surge. The day rounds off with a phone call from social services to confirm the meeting; this is taken by the carer.

All the details are agreed and they look forward to seeing Susan in the morning. That call, made with the best intentions, was only a confirmation of the appointment. To Susan it was affirmation that she *has* to attend tomorrow and there is no way out for her. The scale now reaches level 6.

The next morning after another bad night, she is up, washed and dressed. Even her favourite breakfast and television show have not calmed her nerves. The scale is 6.5 pushing level 7.

Susan has her carer for support. The bus arrives on time, which is good, but on board is a man who Susan does not like. The man has never spoken to her, but he always smells of a strong aftershave that overpowers her senses. For most of the journey the smell continues until he gets off at the stop before hers; the stench makes her nauseous. The scale is rising from level 7 to 8.

Susan arrives on time, which is good. The social worker is there to meet them which is also good, but the centre is noisy today and the sun shines very brightly through the windows. This is painful and hurts her eyes and ears. The level is now 8.5 and Susan is starting to shake.

As they all walk to the room, the lad who 'bullies' Susan comes charging down the corridor to see the social worker, who he likes a lot. He has no intention of interacting in any way with Susan.

This is unknown to Susan, who simply sees danger. Fear descends and a flight response kicks in. Panic has overtaken; the scale is at 10. There is nothing further for Susan to do but immediately withdraw in the other direction.

She runs out of the front door into the road narrowly avoiding your patrol vehicle, which you have to bring to a halt sharply. Susan is rooted to the spot in the middle of the road causing mayhem. You now have to deal with her and two weeks worth of anxiety. How do you do it?

DEBRIEF

The example has been designed to demonstrate how something that seems trivial can impact so heavily on a person with autism. There are lots of things in the above that are good but can be perceived as bad by an autistic person. Anxiety is potentially lethal if left unheeded. As professional people, you can dictate how the environment into which you bring/take them will impact on their senses. Noisy, brightly lit, small places may have a negative impact on the person.

Environmental impact will be dealt with in depth later on but for now just thinking ahead about where you take an autistic person may be the difference between a successful encounter or not.

Also, when you encounter an autistic person who is in shutdown like Susan or Eddie, the first thing that you must consider after autism has leapt into your mind is how to keep the person safe in that environment. This can be by assisting them to a safer place or making them feel safe.

Stress

The above can also be attributed to stress.

Stress is the body's way of responding to any kind of demand or threat. When it senses danger, which can be real or perceived, the body's defences automatically spring into action, producing the archetypal 'fight or flight' response.

Autistic people are often in a heightened state of anxiety or stress due to the environment they are in, which is very draining emotionally and physically. It is this 'heightened' state that can easily escalate depending directly on the way they are dealt with by others.

By adjusting the way you deal with autistic people, you can determine how they feel, react and cope with the sudden extra stresses placed upon their fragile emotions. By just stepping back out of their immediate space (which is not always possible or desirable) you can relieve some of the load on their already overloaded system.

Do not assume that silence is calmness. Far from it: the exterior lack of emotion can be the most dangerous sign. It can indicate that there has been a sensory shutdown resulting from over-stimulation. That in turn can put such extreme strains on the body it can result in seizures.

At all times watch what the person is doing. Eyes can be a clear indicator for what is happening internally. As with intoxicants, the pupils can contract or dilate. Ask yourself why. Better still, ask them. Do not be afraid to enquire what *they* feel, *how* they are or *what* is going on inside them. Some may not be able to verbalise it, others will.

Above all, treat the person with autism as a *human being*. Give them the respect you would want for yourself. They deserve this at the very minimum.

Anger

This is an appropriate point to consider anger: it is this emotion that may bring an autistic person into direct contact with you. Whether it is in their home or in a public space, a person with autism can find themselves being angry all too easily just as an NT person can.

Feeling angry is just part of being alive. It can be in response to any number of things, such as being insulted, jostled or frustrated. In modern times, it seems that anger is more prevalent than at any time in our history.

Some autistic people become angry or aggressive very quickly and find it hard to deal with. The speed and intensity with which they become angry can seem extreme, but when considered in the context of their anxiety, is then understandable.

When feeling angry, autistic people explain they find it hard to unlock themselves from the anger and think of alternative strategies to resolve the situation. It is as if the anger has become the reason for feeling the way they do and all else has subsided.

This is not dissimilar from a neurotypical response. The 'red mist' will descend over the NT person and their actions are completely consumed in that moment. Many acts of violence have been explained away to this reaction.

How it differs in autism is the speed at which it can suddenly seem to appear on a routine basis. It will be the anxiety that leads to the anger. Stemming from this instant panic they will have no safety valve, which prevents an outward aggression. But it will not usually be directed at you; it is rather an automatic response to protect themselves. They will not be gaining any satisfaction from doing something like this in the way an NT offender might. Again, after having read the anxiety section, you can now see how the environment and situation have a direct effect on the person with autism. Relieve the stress, relieve the anger.

Once angry, it can be extremely difficult for an autistic person to let go of that anger. Rational thinking seems to have melted and all they are left with is a raging inferno. Strategies that can be adopted to assist them vary immensely.

Autistic people can suffer with these flashes of anger and as with anxiety it can be present before they have any realisation that it is there. A calm environment, somewhere they feel safe and comfortable, can be the only place where it can be extinguished.

Being in the same places again may cause the anger to come back as before, effectively pushing the same 'triggers', so they will try to avoid them. Autism does not come with many internal 'precursors', so they are usually at level 9 or 10 before they have time to react. No matter what strategies have been taught, anger can be upon an autistic person before they know it.

Having dealt with anger in many environments, and from my understanding of the autistic brain, this may be a strange concept to accept but, if you verbally acknowledge that the autistic person is angry and you understand how hard that is to deal with, you could see them relax slightly.

It may not happen but, having someone recognise their anger and simply accept it can be immediately disarming. It may take the wind out of their sails. They don't want to be angry but have found themselves there. Being spoken to civilly can work wonders.

As I have said, these are not magic spells to stop a situation but nuggets of information to add to your steadily growing toolbox. It all goes to add to the wealth of knowledge about autism that you are hopefully gaining.

How it will affect you as an officer is the important matter and how you deal with it is crucial. The first step is recognising it and knowing what to look out for, including non-verbal communications (NVCs) and traits. These can be very similar to anyone else becoming angry, but with autism it can be harder to spot if the person is already stimming or flapping.

As you would do when dealing with anyone you do not know, watch the autistic person's body language:

- Are their hand movements increasing?
- Have the hands gone from tapping to clenching?
- Is the rocking momentum getting faster?
- Is their breathing increasing?
- Is the pitch of the noise they are making becoming higher or faster?
- Are they now grimacing?

Once you are at this stage, you should now be switched on and backing away slightly (if possible). Whatever is happening in this immediate environment is causing this anger to rise. Remember the anxiety gauge: this is exactly the same. The only way it differs is the speed at which anger can rise, as if the increments are much closer together. The person with autism may not be able to convey they are becoming angry; it can be such a powerful rush of emotion that it is upon them before they can react. Be fully aware of this important fact.

When dealing with autism, always think of anger within the person. Not because it is always there but if you do everything you can to prevent it, this will help them remain calmer. Keep to the Golden Rules I introduce later and you should be able to contain the situation.

Most of the time, the autistic person will simply want to go home to where they feel safe and not want any interaction with you. It is the fact that you are detaining them in that place, at that time and doing that thing that will start the anxiety/anger scale moving. Keep calm, stick to my plans and all should go well.

Sensory overload

When you are called to an incident involving a person with autism the first thing you may encounter is lack of communication or response, or non-compliance. Amongst all of the things I have already discussed it can also be a sign of sensory overload (SO).

SO occurs when one or more of the body's senses experiences over-stimulation from the environment around it. SO can be a result of many impact factors.

Lights, smells, temperature and noise can all be hidden from the person dealing with the incident but be overwhelming to the autistic person. It can take just one, but more usually there will be a mixture of attacks on their senses. A phrase I use is 'environmental impact' as it will be all of the things around them that are impacting on them. It will be overpowering and completely beyond their control. Rather than ignoring you, the individual or suspect may not know how or even be unable to communicate beyond this barrage.

Hands slapped over their ears or eyes are a definite sign of sensory overload.

Do not try to remove them.

In doing so you are taking away the only protection they've put in place to stop an invasion into their body. Instead, try to enter the space around them and use the back-up techniques from this book to reassure them you mean no extra harm.

The most likely way you will see a sensory overload is if you attend someone displaying aggressive behaviour. This visual sign will almost certainly be down to a rise in anxiety. This emotional outburst will probably have nothing to do with you but your presence could make it worse if handled insensitively.

It is an automatic (trained?) response from an officer to want to obtain immediate cooperation. Without compliance do you feel at a disadvantage? The natural response to someone uncooperative is to go 'hands on'.

At this point, STOP, step back and re-evaluate.

These simple but unnatural actions for an officer could potentially be life-saving to the individual they are dealing with.

A common misconception is that autistic people are predominantly non-communicative. The vast majority of the autistic people you will be called to or an even higher percentage you encounter on the streets will be quite able to communicate but may feel unable to speak due to sensory overload or, more likely, fear.

The obligation lies squarely with *you* to establish a comfortable enough situation to enable communication, not for the individual you encounter to adapt to your demands.

Rocking back and forth, finger clicking, humming, singing and drawing patterns in the air are all signs of stimming. The repetition of physical movements or sounds, or constant movement of objects may be annoying or distracting for you, but stimming is a perfectly benign activity and can allow the person with autism to communicate whilst they are doing it or can act as a form of communication itself. It can also be a way of trying to calm themselves down. Their carer can be useful in these situations to interpret their behaviour.

Working sensitively with them rather than stopping the actions will definitely be more productive and could provide a more peaceful resolution to the situation.

Triggers, dislikes and allures

These are the three most common areas you will come into contact with when encountering an autistic person. Let me explain the difference between dislikes and triggers.

A dislike is something you will be more readily able to identify with, as everyone has dislikes. However where the NT person can filter the problem out of the equation, sometimes quite successfully, an autistic person will not be able to. It is more than not liking something; for them it will be a revulsion and it will quite possibly be visible to you. They may turn away from the source of this dislike or put their hands up to put some distance between them and it. More signs could be pulling away or even running off. They will want to be as far away from the source as possible. It could be *you* that is causing this adverse reaction, even the clothes you are wearing, including your uniform.

Imagine the most fearful thing you can, your darkest fear. If you were confronted by this, I am willing to bet you would not be able to stand and calmly deal with it. An easy example is a summer's day in the garden; you are standing with a fizzy drink in your hand and several large wasps attack you, zoning in on the drink. Your natural instinct would be to run away swatting at them or even throw your drink down to divert them away from you. These are rational fears because the large wasps are quite capable of stinging you and it will hurt, a lot.

Now, apply this newfound understanding to the autistic person in front of you. The quick movement away from you suddenly makes sense. Their previously inexplicable yanking from your grasp or turning their head sharply away or even simply not making eye contact with you can all be explained quite easily now.

The behaviour you see is the primitive 'fight or flight' you will hopefully have been taught about in the early lessons in the self-defence classes. It is the 'flinch' response that is inside all of us. Just look at any picture of a footballer heading a ball and they are invariably closing their eyes at some point during the procedure. This hardwired action is just as powerful with autistic people. The thing that is scaring, upsetting or hurting them is causing them to seek refuge *immediately*. It is not something they have any control over, the same as you do not. You may see this as defiance or even as an attempt to escape from lawful custody and it very well may not be. If you are shouting at them, touching them or invading their personal space then:

STOP. THINK. Is this person autistic?

A trigger is an unplanned instance that hits your memory bank and opens the flood gates, allowing the original incident free to invade your present situation. It is possibly like a flashback. It can come via any of the senses but the easiest to explain is a smell.

Most people agree that freshly cut grass stimulates some strong memory, usually pleasant and possibly from childhood. For an autistic person it could be that exact smell that suddenly causes them to retch or even vomit. It really is that powerful. They have no control over the reaction in the same way you will jump at a loud bang.

So, the trigger you may see from the autistic person when you interact with them is completely automatic and they will have no control over how they react. A classic symptom that will be obvious is freezing to the spot. It may come across as ignorance or avoidance but a complete shutdown is a common reaction.

If an autistic person has come into contact with something that has caused them to have an adverse reaction to a dislike or trigger, it may be that you have been called to deal with the incident. In public there are numerous things which could affect them and the way they react can be seen by NT people as completely unwarranted or even bizarre. When attending a scene, if you see the detained person trying to make themselves as small as possible, retching or refusing to look at you, before you grab them or shout at them for not doing as you have demanded:

STOP. THINK. Are they autistic?

They might well be in the worst environment possible for them. Think back to that wasp attack or your worst fear; this may be theirs. Give the person with autism thinking time, reassure them and above all be patient. Trying to fight fear is a difficult process; making added demands of them will only make the situation worse. Also take charge of the space you are in. Control the person who has called you as they may want immediate action. Tell them you are dealing with the incident as *you* see fit. Give the autistic person all the chances you would wish for yourself. To deal with any vulnerable person in this manner is how the job should be carried out and will hopefully be beneficial to all parties in the end.

At this point I will mention 'allures' – these are things that have a powerful attraction.

An autistic person may like something so much they can find it irresistible or be unable to stop themselves from becoming obsessed by it to such a point that they must have it (also see the addiction section below for further explanation). The autistic person may have found the allure so powerful that their actions have brought them into criminality to obtain the object of their desire. If you find yourself dispatched to a case where this is mentioned please stop and consider the possibility of autism. Speak with the carer and see why the crime has occurred (if at all) and explore all options before 'criminalising' the autistic person.

Triggers, dislikes and allures can all be distressing, but are physically draining. Having to negotiate the path of the senses is tiring for autistic people. Understand this when you are dealing with them; they are working much harder than you simply to be in the outside world.

Think of your central nervous system being on ultra-sensitive mode, constantly. It is impacting on them all of the time and stays with them long after an incident has passed. If you are suddenly alarmed by a noise, you will calm very quickly and carry on with your life. For an autistic person it can feel as though their nerves have been shredded, a feeling which will not go away. Like the action of fingernails being drawn down a blackboard or chewing on tinfoil, the world around them can be so horrendous it forces them to withdraw to somewhere safe, where they can finally relax.

The next example deals with one of these 'allures' in a manner which you may not have considered.

EXAMPLE 3

Francis is in his late 30s and has always had a love for birds of prey. Ever since finding a kestrel with a broken wing when he was 9, he has cared for and loved many species, some of which he has in an aviary at the bottom of his garden.

He has longed to work as a keeper at the local wildlife rescue centre, but he is too shy and lacks confidence. Whilst at an open day, he hears that the raptor section (all predatory birds) is closed due to the recent outbreak of Canker (a bird digestive condition).

Francis is naturally upset, as he has waited all year to see his favourite animals. He knows Canker does not affect humans. He has read all about it and if he does not touch anything, he will be okay.

He is spotted on CCTV entering the restricted area. When challenged by staff he refuses to accompany them away from the dangers. Eventually the stand-off warrants police presence.

Consider how you would deal with Francis.

DEBRIEF

Francis *must* see the birds of prey. He cannot resist going to their enclosure. In his mind, he is doing nothing wrong; he knows all about the disease and how to deal with it. The only thing he is technically doing wrong is civil trespass. He has his hands in his pockets. He feels he is safe. The staff are only trying to protect him and want him to leave but he can't do that until he has seen all of the birds.

Notice I have used *can't* instead of *won't*. It isn't that he is simply having a 'strop'; in his mind there will be no other alternative. Remember autistic people can have very rigid mindsets. He is not being awkward or defiant, he is genuinely there to 'visit' the raptors. It is a logical and simple train of thought. Do not become annoyed that autistic people are at odds with the request being made of them.

STOP. THINK AUTISM.

An easy way to deal with this situation would be to simply grab Francis and yank him out of the area. You have been told it is distressing for the birds to have an unknown visitor. He is trespassing and you have little time to deal with this. Job done.

STOP. REASSESS.

With a little rethinking, could you perhaps speak to the staff and negotiate a revisit for Francis when the birds are better? Explain this to him, be patient, perhaps even try to use his love of birds to ease the way.

'You don't want the birds to suffer do you, Francis? They are scared because they do not know you. Why not come back and let the staff show you around and introduce you to the birds then, eh?'

This is a small price to pay for a peaceful exit. Think of other options. *Do not* go hands on unless you absolutely have to.

When called to something of this nature, start with:

Is the person autistic?

Think about what you are hearing and listen to what you are being told. Does this make sense to you? Is what is happening in front of you usually what you expect to investigate? If there seems no criminal intent, then automatically escalate to autism. People like Francis exist everywhere; they may have different interests or hobbies but their passion and intensity will be the same. They may pop up in any situation where their logical approach can be misconstrued as suspicious or criminal when it simply isn't, like the one above.

Stay calm, think clearly, use the Golden Rules below and you will have a much greater chance of an equitable solution.

Addiction

Addiction is defined as:

not having control over doing, taking or using something to the point where it could be harmful to you.

You can become addicted to almost anything. Some of the most common are drugs (illegal or prescription), alcohol and nicotine.

Whatever an autistic person is doing may seem completely harmless to them and is certainly not illegal (scratch cards or online gambling for instance) but it is the force that drives them to do this that can lead them into criminality.

A lot of autistic people follow rules happily; this fulfils their ordered lives. The thought of breaking rules can be quite repellant or even intangible. However, if funds become low, they could simply forget the rules to feed the habit. Worse still, their vulnerability leaves them open to persuasion or a friendly whisper in the ear (see mate crime later) to commit crime in order to fund the addiction.

Some people with autism have a deep desire to feel satisfied, in as much as they have an inbuilt predilection to become attached to certain objects, programmes or foods to name a few. They can obsess about TV shows or characters, watching them endlessly. If something is deliberately offered to them in order to ensnare that hunger, then it is at this point they will most likely become embroiled with the law. In whichever way the autistic person has arrived at the addiction, it is how the officer deals with them that is crucial.

The first question to be answered is, did they know what they did was illegal? The officer may need to break this down into smaller steps: was the thing bad? Was it against any rules they know? Do they know it is wrong to steal, burgle or even rob someone? If the genuine answer is no, then further work with the carer must be carried out in order to find out what led them to the point of breaking the law.

As I highlighted above, do not assume every autistic person is unaware of the law; some will be only too knowledgeable of the system, but choose to 'play' innocent. Background work done with the carer should furnish you with the truth.

How to recognise autism

There is still a belief amongst the populace that all autistic people are basically the same: that they conform to stereotypical traits, behave in a similar way and like the same things.

This misnomer stems from a complete lack of understanding about autism and outdated concepts that can easily be dispelled by those of us with autism, finally speaking up in our defence.

The statement below is therefore clear and unequivocal:

Every autistic person is different. They will present differently and require a different strategy to assist them.

Furthermore, just as one may stim another may not. One might recoil from touch, another might enjoy it. Keep an open mind and assess each situation with new eyes.

As mentioned previously, the autism can easily present as someone in drink (a police term for being intoxicated by alcohol), intoxicated by drugs or suffering from mental health issues. All four of these are not mutually exclusive and research has shown a high proportion of repeat offenders in the CJS cross over several categories. Drink and drugs can lead to mental health issues; conversely they can be used to relieve them. The same can be said about autism. An autistic adult has just as much access (some even more) to alcohol or drugs due to their vulnerability, which ultimately can lead to mental health issues.

When you are confronted by someone who seems to fit these criteria, the alcohol, drug or mental health issues must be considered and ruled out individually when assessing for autism. If you are in doubt then seek the help of a health care professional as soon as possible.

A person with autism certainly will not be walking around with a neon sign above their head which lights up and flashes saying 'Autistic!' when you approach them. They will be just like anyone else in the crowd. However, when you are dealing with someone there could be signs to tell you they could be autistic.

Some more subtle indications a person may be autistic are:

- They may have trouble keeping up a conversation on your terms or be prone to long speeches on their favourite subject. They may not be avoiding your questions but filling the gaps in the conversation by using something they know a lot about. Do not treat this as being cheeky.

- They may not be able to contain their emotions in a stressful situation. This could be as simple as the act of you talking to them. Not everyone likes talking to the police and this may be the very first time they have met a police officer. Be aware of this and be patient.

- What they say and how they look to you may be completely at odds. They may say they are okay and their voice be calm but be at breaking point on the inside. They may be shouting and seem aggressive but be panicking on the inside. Do not assume anything. Seek further information from the situation.

- Facial expressions, body language, gestures or social cues usually employed in the communication process may be unclear to them. To an autistic person your face may be completely blank. No matter how you screw it up, nod, wink or grin, they may not be able to read anything on it. This does not mean they are stupid, far from it; there is simply no ability to see the differences in people's faces. Think about when you have a heavy cold; your sense of smell is missing but it does not make you any less of a person. It is the same with body language or social clues: the mechanisms that are present for NT people were not created at birth for the neurodiverse. Do not expect them to instantly react to something you take for granted. If at first you do not receive an answer to your gestures then try and be direct and ask them openly, but be polite. It is not their fault; it is up to you to facilitate this process rather than it being a problem for them to decipher.

- They may engage in repetitive behaviours whilst in your presence. This can be a whole host of actions as previously mentioned in SSB, such as stimming (tapping, spinning objects etc.). Again, this is nothing personal against you. The fact they are using these behaviours can be a positive for you instead of a negative; consider that. For an autistic person who has limited verbal responses (be that only in stressful situations) then this outward action can be their only way to communicate and the fact they are trying to reach out to you means you must be aware of it. If possible, always seek confirmation from someone who knows them, but if they are not available, STOP. THINK. Why are they doing this and *how* can I help lower their anxiety?

- They may have a deeper knowledge of one particular subject (a special interest: SI) and may not want to talk about anything else. Should you be lucky enough to be in a conversation with a person with autism then do not try to confuse them with complicated questions. Be direct and if they do start to launch into a long speech about their favourite subject matter or specific interest then please listen to them for a short while and then gently steer them back to the reason you are there. They are not being rude. This may be the best day of their life, having a police officer all to themselves, so enjoy it for that brief period.

- They may become distressed when changes occur in their daily routines, which in turn cause them anxiety. A change of routine – be that a meal, item of clothing or route to the shops – can be the worst thing that has happened to a person with autism at that moment. Think back to Eddie standing in the railway station when the platform change is announced. The inability to control their world can be extremely upsetting for them and lead to unwanted anxiety. It may be this incident that has brought them to your attention, if someone has reported their strange behaviour (be it rocking back and forward in the town centre or screaming on a bus). Be aware they are not being unreasonable or childish. It will feel to them as if they are spinning out of control and have nothing to hold onto. Be patient and seek the cause of the anxiety. Remember that lowering the anxiety may enable the person to re-engage with you.

- Whereas an NT will understand what is required from the situation and say what is expected of them, an autistic person may not. If the autistic person you are dealing with does not seem to be getting what you are saying, try rephrasing it. The onus is squarely upon your shoulders to make the conversation/interview or stop-check flow as smoothly as possible, not on theirs to understand all of your nuances.

- There may be a lack of eye contact from the autistic person. Some autistic people do not like to make eye contact; it makes them feel vulnerable, scared or may even be painful. In others it is not such a problem. It is down to how the individual feels. Do not try to reposition yourself to make it impossible for them to avoid your gaze as this will make them feel even more anxious. For a long time, it has been used as an indicator when assessing for autism. During the flow of conversation between neurotypical people, certain things can occur naturally. These can be facial expressions, intonation of voice and eye contact. Nothing is thought about these interactions, until one of them is missing. So much has been made of this tiny part of a person's overall make-up that to some it has become the 'holy grail' of autism. Making eye contact is not a problem for me, as over the years I was trained to watch people's eyes, which can be a precursor to any number of unwanted actions by a perpetrator. Due to this 'talent' I have worked hard to perfect in order to fit in, professionals I worked with used it as a clear sign that I could not be autistic. You can now start to see the problems faced by many autistic people, having to justify their life against a set of diagnostic criteria.

If any or all of these are present when you are speaking to someone then it should start to form an indication that the person may be autistic. They are not absolute certainties, however if several of them are present, deal with that person as if they were autistic. If you are wrong, being careful and understanding will never harm a situation.

Criminal behaviour or autism?

Right from the start you as a police officer are trained to look out for suspicious behaviour and whether the person you are dealing with is dubious or not. It is this very thing that makes the bobby what they are. You are taught to identify what is wrong with a situation and which are the red flags that need investigating.

The following are just a few red flags that may cause you to stop and speak to a person with autism:

- avoiding eye contact with the officer or zero eye contact throughout the whole interaction

- flippant responses to questions asked by the officer

- unusual or strange replies

- becoming agitated during questions

- the pitch (e.g. shouty), tone (may come across as aggressive) or volume (too loud) of their speech

- being out late at night (in a particular area or all alone)

- staring at the officer or inappropriate looks during questioning

- appearing too calm when spoken to

- talking too much/being hyperactive

- lack of compliance with the procedure

- looking like they are drunk, clumsy or staggering

- monotone answers

- shifting feet whilst being spoken to

- inappropriate clothing (in general and for the time of year)

- oblivious to the presence of the officer

- ignoring the officer's approach

- no answers at all or seemingly refusing to respond

- being protective over items they are carrying.

By choosing just a few from the list you would start to take notice of someone in front of you; I certainly would. These types of behaviour are the classic ones that are drummed into us as police officers when we were at college or out with our tutors and they stay with you for the rest of your life (not just as a copper). That 'gut feeling' that you cannot explain but nags at you and provides the adrenaline to carry out your job is created by all of these markers above. However it is exactly these that are echoed by autism.

The following are prime examples of how an autistic person can become ensnared in the CJS and end up being imprisoned after being failed by the system at every stage. Look at them and see if you recognise anything.

A stop-check of someone because of their suspicious behaviour may result in you speaking to an autistic person. The way autism presents to police officers will often result in their further detention due to the unusual replies given to your questions. Literal thinking is far more than just taking what you say at face value or comprehending idioms as factual; their responses to your regulated questions can seem to be disrespectful or even insulting and could result in an arrest.

A visible or public outburst is something that will bring the autistic person to your attention and possible arrest. A lot of autistic people have a need for routine in order to reduce their anxieties. They may need to do the same thing every day or walk the same route each time and when this routine is disrupted it causes a sharp rise in their anxiety, stress or a sensory overload, which is causing the reaction that you are called to deal with.

The damage you see around you upon arrival may have been caused by the autistic person but is also a by-product of the stress they are under. Their actions may not have any conscious connection to an offence and they may have no idea that it has been caused by them.

When you place a hand on their shoulder to calm them down or restrain they can rear up or push you away. This obvious 'resist arrest' is actually their inbuilt defence mechanism. Some autistic people really cannot stand to be touched at all. Your grip can feel like a burning sensation to their flesh or a searing pain. The need to escape your touch is just that: a 'must' not a mild dislike. At that point all their body is trying to do is get as far away from the source as possible. This will display as an attempt to escape custody and resist arrest but will certainly not be.

Their fight to free themselves will almost certainly continue all the way to custody where they are seen by fresh eyes as a screaming banshee and further restrained and confined. They may not be able to fully recover from this incident at all whilst in custody. Their anxiety will be off the scale and their ability to engage will be minimal at best. This makes the autistic person extremely vulnerable throughout their entire time in police detention.

Interviewing then may seem a doddle. They may answer all of your questions with a yes or nod. They may have rejected legal advice and most certainly not had an AA as their autism will not have been detected. Autistic people can have a fear or awe of the police and will do anything you ask to please you. Being vulnerable is more than just not understanding social clues; they may genuinely not understand why they are there at all. The rights that have been read to them mean little or nothing to them.

If at the point of charge they are bailed with conditions not to visit the shop they were arrested in, for instance, they may flatly refuse. This unusual reaction should also flag up autism. Again rigidity of mind can mean that they have no other alternatives. Being placed before the courts for just this type of behaviour is not unusual. At court they may still refuse legal advice because they have no clue what a solicitor is. The court then has no option but to remand as they steadfastly refuse to engage and abide by these conditions. Finally whilst on remand someone from the prison services identifies their autism and they receive the right intervention that was required from the start.

Why it has taken this long to have intervention is down to a lack of autism awareness right across the CJS. At any point someone with autism training could have seen that this individual is obviously vulnerable and in dire need of help. This book contains all of the clues required to identify autism at all stages of the CJS right from first spotting something suspicious.

When you are next out on patrol and see something suspicious and the person seems not to fit your criteria:

STOP. THINK. Is this autism?

Chapter 2

How to deal with autism

I have talked about the Golden Rules but until now have not revealed them. The reason for this is that, without all of the other background information, their use would be linear. Now you have been through several scenarios and learned what to do the hard way, and more importantly what not to do, the rules will simply slot in alongside the other tips you have picked up, meaning much more than if they had been shouted at you on page one.

The Golden Rules

1. STOP!

2. STAND BACK.

3. ASSESS THE SITUATION.

4. STAY CALM AT ALL TIMES.

5. SPEAK SLOWLY AND MORE CLEARLY.

6. DO NOT USE SLANG OR LONG WORDS. KEEP IT SIMPLE.

7. DO NOT TOUCH THE PERSON UNLESS YOU HAVE TO, I.E. TO ARREST/SEARCH.

8. CHECK FOR ANY FORM OF ID. ID in this case includes an autism card, family phone number, carer's contact details or a phone with information on it.

Using the Golden Rules at all times will enable you to deal with autistic people far more effectively. They have been designed to be easy to understand and simple to carry out. Learn them, even carry a copy of them with you to pull out and refresh your memory. If you are sent to a job involving a person with autism or if you feel the person may be autistic employing these strategies could be invaluable to you.

Initial contact with an autistic person

I have worked with the autistic community and they told me how they have been treated by the police and how they wished they had been treated. There are a few good examples of police work, however in the main it wasn't a positive experience for them.

When you deal with any member of the public you are taught to take control of the situation and direct the encounter confidently. This will cause a different reaction with a person with autism, as already outlined.

It is all about managing *your* expectations of the person you are dealing with. If you suspect autism, take your time, use small steps and be patient. By using these strategies you will be enabling the autistic person to communicate on the same equal terms as anyone else. Here are a few more quick bullet points to help you when dealing with autistic people:

- Ask one question or give only one instruction at a time.

- Processing an instruction can take up to 10 seconds; wait this long, count in your head if necessary.

- If repeating an instruction use exactly the *same* words and tone of voice.

- STOP. Repeat the second bullet point.

- *Do not* become frustrated or lose your temper. This is counter-productive.

- Try to find a common ground if you can. Observe what they are wearing/carrying; a t-shirt, rucksack, comic or toy may have a character you can use to engage them. Autistic people sometimes have special interests (SI), which they will only be too happy to talk about given the right environment.

- Treat them with the respect you would want for yourself.

I want to break these down further and explain a little more about speaking clearly.

It is more than just enunciating properly. It is the way we form a sentence in the mind before allowing it to be heard. Constructing unambiguous conversation is not what the modern NT world is all about. These days, there are far more instances of 'text speak' and abbreviations contained within conversation than ever before. If you think of the 'Pathé News' announcer or the old radio broadcasters, you'll remember that language then was clipped and precise. One knew what to say and how to say it. Now it has become sloppy and slang-drenched. It is full of nuances that an autistic person can easily miss or overlook due to a more literal understanding of language.

Language is confusing enough without police-speak being ladled onto it. When you join the constabulary, the new terms and acronyms are exciting because you are learning a code, a secret language. Using it every day leads to an entrenched lexicon, which is perfectly fine for the people you work with but it means nothing to the larger demographic. Police officers often use it without even knowing it; their slang is quite clear to them but the people they encounter are sometimes left confused or even offended by what they interpret from the terms.

Think about how you speak when you address an autistic person even if they appear to be verbally able. Talk as if they are a foreign visitor and you are directing them to somewhere. You would not say to a tourist, 'Go down the alley, throw a left at the bottom and if you get lost do a u-ee an mosey back to the bollards, then straight over.' This would result in a blank look. You would actually say slowly, 'Walk to the end of the road, turn left at the end, the theatre is 100 metres on the right.'

It is exactly the same with autism. Be clear, be patient.

Only ask one question at a time: 'What is your name?' Wait for a few seconds, then if you have no response, look closely at them and see if they are thinking or they are not engaging. They do not have to engage, after all it is a free world. The only time they may have to follow an order or instruction is when being told to do so for their own safety or someone else's, such as a firearms incident.

If you receive a fairly quick response to your first question, pause, then ask the next. Don't bombard them with questions, one after the other. It will be a confusing time for them; stress can block the senses. Be patient.

If you ask an autistic person a question or give an instruction, the reason you use the same words if you repeat it stems from the first two stages above. There will still be a processing time. Your words may enter their mind and join the others, which will reinforce the first command. Using other words will simply confuse them and be processed as another question, starting the process all over again. It will be quicker for you and easier for them.

For example:

You ask, 'Can you tell me your name?'

Reply: 'Yes.'

This may immediately seem to be insolence, it isn't.

Try, 'What is your name?'

Reply: 'Peter.'

Wait. Then you ask, 'What are you doing here?' This is a reasonable question.

Reply: 'Talking to you.'

Once again, this is *not* them being cheeky. Use even more patience.

Ask, 'What were you doing before I stopped you?'

Reply: 'Going to the shop over there,' and they point to the newspaper shop across the road.

By using simple, clear questions you have succeeded in preventing this autistic person possibly getting arrested. You have not perceived their answers as being cheeky and evading the truth but now you see how they have given you the correct answers in a far more easy way.

If you misconstrue an answer it can so quickly deteriorate a reasonable interaction and result in the person with autism being detained further to satisfy the original perception of guilt. It has happened more times than I can count, all over the world, on a daily basis. Autistic people give an officer a seemingly wrong answer to an overly complicated question and end up being arrested for doing nothing wrong. Stay calm and take time to decipher what you have been told.

On the back of this I am now going onto another area that can also come across as criminal or more often disrespectful. Look at it carefully as you may have already experienced it without even knowing it.

Echolalia

A person standing in front of you repeating your words or using random phrases when you are speaking to them may seem to be a deliberate act to annoy you. However, echolalia is an automatic response and the thoughts and actions behind these words can be just as important as the rest of their presentation to you.

Echolalia can be the immediate repetition of the last word or words you say, creating a buffer or space for the autistic person to answer your question. It can happen purely out of panic as the body produces the easiest response. Be aware that the more anxiety the person feels, the more echolalia you could be faced with.

From personal experience I do it and have no control over it at all. I hear a noise and repeat it as it makes me feel good inside. Most of the time it is out before I can stop it. In another way it can be a word I hear and simply need to repeat, for no reason at all. It is out and gone, never to return. Or it can make me feel more secure in a stressful situation where I repeat the word or noise on a loop, hundreds of times. Whatever it is, autistic people do it and it is nearly always a reaction to the environment they are in and not aimed at you.

When speaking to an autistic person it may seem that they are being cheeky or trying to goad you. Listen to what they have just said and try to flip the question around to see if you get the same answer. This advice can particularly be useful in an interview or statement situation and even more so in a court proceeding.

For instance you ask,

'Did they ask you to stay in or go out?'

'Go out.'

'Did they ask you to go out or stay in?'

'Stay in.'

In this example the person is simply repeating the last words. It may seem that they are avoiding answering the question but they may just be hearing the last few words and repeating them as it is the expected response.

It may be that the person mimics exactly what you say in the exact tone or inflection. Again this may not be designed to offend but something they cannot stop. Try to stay calm and be patient with your questioning.

The echolalia may be immediate, as in the repetition of your last words, or it could be delayed and be from their memory banks. The delay could be from an hour, day or even years previously. Something you have said will have triggered a memory of those words and can be taken from a film, TV series or a book. The use of the word or words can release stimulation internally and be extremely satisfying for them.

It could be from their favourite film and they have been waiting to say it from the moment they heard it. They know exactly how it should be delivered and will not stop until it has been.

This might come across as being flippant but take a minute to digest the quote; it could be a throw away comment but may actually have some bearing on the case. It could be that the person opposite you has a million quotes and is only too happy to unleash them at will. Be careful in responding with a quote of your own as they may see it as a challenge and have done it for hours with people they know. Keep the interview/statement on track with an unrelated question from your list.

For example, during a burglary interview you ask the detainee:

'When you entered the building, you didn't expect them to be there, did you?'

They reply in a louder than expected voice, 'Nobody expects the Spanish Inquisition. Our chief weapon is surprise!'

This is a quote from the *Monty Python's Flying Circus* TV series and has been overly used for many years. However the use of it in a serious environment such as a police interview should immediately alert you (if not noted before) to the proposition that the person sitting opposite you may be autistic.

They have picked up on just one word, 'expect', and used it to deliver this classic line. Rather than asking them why they have just said it, ignoring it and asking the original question in a different way could get the answer you want:

'Did you think the security guards would still be there when you entered the building?'

'No.'

This way you have given the person time to process the question again and they are back on track with your interview and calm enough to answer your questions. Going head to head with them could cause the anxiety to rise and produce even more irrelevant quotes, which will be destructive for all involved.

Another part of delivering a line or quote is that once it has been done, the user may genuinely have no memory of saying it. As it has come from the deep memory area of the brain, it may have by-passed the short term area and have returned to whence it came. Do not be alarmed by a lack of recognition if you mention it; they might not be able to recall it happening.

Echolalia can be the repetition of noises too. If an alarm goes off it can be that the person will repeat it. The same goes for sirens, ringtones or loud noises such as bangs or crashes. The stimulation could be the fear of the sudden noise or it may feel pleasant to that person.

Whether immediate or delayed, echolalia is an important issue if encountered. If the person with autism's carer is present, then you may wish to ask if there is anything you can do to circumnavigate this behaviour. If there is nothing to be done, try to work around how the questions are being answered and possibly use any knowledge of the subject the quote has come from or slow the questions down to give the person more time to process them. It really could be as simple as that.

Also, finding a common ground is something you will do automatically when meeting someone for the first time.

Your shared experiences make the conversation flow more easily and create a pleasant experience. Use this thought for dealing with a person with autism. They may have a special interest in something that is quite visible to you. If they are wearing a Pokémon™ t-shirt or carrying a tiger rucksack, then take notice of this. Talk to them about it. You don't have to have intimate knowledge of it; they will be more than happy to enlighten you, given the chance. Ask them a question about it, 'Wow, that's a cool t-shirt. What's Pokémon™?' You could even reinforce the question by pointing to it.

Again wait for the reply, as this may have brought something new to the table: shyness. They may have been teased about it or feel so protective about their favourite subject that it may take time to build up trust to speak about it.

Trust is a simple concept but it has to be earned. Just because you are in uniform it does not mean you get it for free. Spend time on the groundwork before you expect a flow of conversation.

During an interaction with any person a useful adage is to treat them with the respect they deserve or treat them how you would like to be treated. No one likes to be shouted at or abused; why would they? This is even more important when dealing with a person with autism.

Why? Autism in itself brings a lot of prejudice. Autistic people are routinely patronised, disregarded and receive daily abuse. From some of the reports I heard, many consider it part of their lives: something to be ignored if possible, endured at best. No one should have to live like that, not in our society. A simple nicety can go such a long way to a vulnerable person. Try it and see.

Remember the oath you took as a police officer: 'I promise to uphold the law without fear or affection, malice or ill will' – tag onto this 'without prejudice'.

When dealing with a person with autism put this into practice and insist all around you do the same.

Stop and search

At some point you will detain an autistic person and the most likely reason will be to stop and search them, but it may also include the recent 'stop and account' provision. As with most members of the public, the autistic person will have no idea that they may be detained by a power under PACE (the Police and Criminal Evidence Act 1984) for the former but not realise there is no lawful power that comes with the latter.

If you are stopping anyone, you will be using all of the training you have received to extract as much information from the detainee as quickly as possible. This may be difficult if the person is autistic. They may appear evasive, uneasy or more nervous than most people. This in itself may raise your level of suspicion enough to move from the account to search. However if you overlay all of my advice on the way you interact with the person, it could become apparent that they are in fact, autistic.

Having stopped and searched many people, the way they responded to me always led to a specific or particular thought pattern in my mind. Aggression and uncooperative behaviour may have led me to be more suspicious but I was far more interested in what lay behind the bravado or evasion.

Autistic people may appear at first to fit many of the criminal stereotypes. So it is extremely important that you use the information in this book to sift swiftly through their responses (or attempt to decipher what an absence of response means if there is none) to get to the reasons behind their behaviour.

Putting your arms out to the side to initially stop the person in a way that shows them that you are preventing them from moving on or attracting their attention may cause them to turn away from you or freeze. Remember this may be the first time they have ever come into contact with a police officer. If you see panic in their eyes or a flinch do not assume they are guilty of something. Be friendly, speak clearly and slow your speech down. Do everything to prevent anxiety rising from the moment you come into contact with any person you encounter and the Golden Rules will assist you in this.

It is likely that you will not be aware that the person you are detaining is autistic until much later in the stop. However, there could be indications already given to suggest they could be. Briefly: panic, rapid breathing, fast talking, becoming rigid, flapping or even stuttering can be early signs the person may be neurodiverse. The way you initially deal with them may have a distinct bearing on how the stop goes. Dealing politely and clearly with everyone you meet is a professional standard by which you should work at the very least.

The next example will show you how this first interaction with someone can change the whole dynamic of a stop and search. Start to employ the techniques you have learned so far to see how you would approach this scenario.

EXAMPLE 4

An officer sees a young man in the street who is clutching a bulky rucksack to his chest by the top handle. This is an unusual method of transportation, which catches their eye. As the young man walks towards the officer, they see a few yards behind him a group of people pointing to the lad. This is sufficient at the very least to speak to him and may be worthy of further investigation.

As the officer stands in the middle of the pavement, they put out their arms to signal for the lad to stop. He does stop but tries to walk around them with his head down.

'Hang on there, matey, what you up to?' they ask but receive no reply, and the lad tries to dart around the other side of them. This behaviour makes the officer suspicious. There have been lots of thefts from the shops in this area over the past few weeks and this could be yet another.

'I said stop! What's in the bag, eh?' They physically prevent him from moving past by placing their right arm out but do not touch him. At this point, they have moved from the area of stop and account into stop and search. The officer feels they have reasonable suspicion of an offence (putting the semantics aside, let us assume the bag contains stolen articles).

The lad freezes but still does not respond to them or look up. After explaining the grounds to detain him, the officer bends their head down to try to get eye contact. The lad simply puts his head down lower and away from their stare.

'What is in the bag?' they ask pointing to it. They receive no reply. The officer feels they have no other avenue but to actually take hold of the bag to search it. When they touch it, the lad snatches it away and shouts, 'No!' at them.

This is sufficient to cause suspicion that the bag does indeed contain stolen or prohibited articles. They take hold of the bag and wrench it away from the lad, placing their other hand on his shoulder to prevent any attack. As the lad is only slight in build, he puts up little actual resistance but is extremely alarmed by their actions and jumps on their arm, encircling the bag with both arms.

The 'quick' look at his bag and a 'chat' have developed into a full-on assault by the lad who is squirming and thrashing around like a freshly landed fish. The officer is struck several times in the melee. They arrest the lad and once cuffed, he is transported and booked into custody, still resisting.

Upon arriving at the custody suite, Joseph is forcibly placed in a cell and the door banged shut. A full search of his bag reveals several books from the local library (from where he had just left); also there was an autism awareness card shoved in the bottom. Upon speaking to the people at the scene, it transpires that they were pointing to Joseph as they had seen him being harassed and bullied by some bigger lads a few seconds before. Having seen the officer, they had run off. The crowd knew Joseph and assumed the officer was coming to help him. Joseph is Aspergic and was clutching the bag to his chest to protect the precious books, as he knew they belonged to someone else and wanted to keep them safe from bullies.

DEBRIEF

You can now see how, by doing something which at first seems quite ordinary and reasonable, the situation descended into an unnecessary arrest and possibly an assault charge, for just a few library books.

By scanning the area a bit more prior to the stop, it could be that the officer saw the other lads running off or they could have tried to steer Joseph to one side before moving onto the next part of the search.

Joseph was scared and wanted to get home as quickly as possible after the bullying incident. Seeing how he was walking towards the officer quite fast, head down and holding the bag in an unusual way could easily have indicated to the officer there was something else behind his actions.

Using the stop and account is not a problem. From the evidence in the scenario, it was a reasonable action. When it began to change from simply a chat to a detention was where the Golden Rules should have been employed.

The officer had plenty of time to formulate a plan before Joseph reached them. Instead of relying just on 'I'm a copper, they will stop because that's the law', they could have tried to engage Joseph before he came within inches of them: 'Hello, I'm PC Bloggs. Are you okay?'

It could be that Joseph was completely unaware of the officer's presence. Do not assume everyone knows who and what you are; tell them, make it obvious.

In this case Joseph was so anxious he may not have been able to respond. He may never have met a police officer before. Whatever the reason:

STOP. STAND BACK. ASSESS.

It may seem completely counterintuitive, dropping to your knees in a busy high street with potential dangers all around you, but in this case it could have been exactly the right decision. Joseph may have been able to see the police uniform and knows they help people in trouble. Also by placing your uniform in

Joseph's sightline you are *not* demanding eye contact but allowing him to look for himself.

I would never advocate placing yourself in any dangerous positions; this is just another angle to use when trying to engage with autistic people. Keep reassuring them of your intentions.

At the first point of contact, Joseph was not a suspect and ultimately never was. So, to save any chance of a complaint, the officer could have said, 'It's okay, I am here to help. What is your name?' The stop and search form clearly requires certain details from the detainee, so the question is both legitimate and non-contentious.

The officer could have repeated their first question again, 'Are you okay?'

If Joseph is not willing to engage or respond then there is little you can do. This will happen and I am not going to suggest every person with autism will magically become pleasant and responsive by just using the Golden Rules. However, look at how the officer is now presenting to Joseph. Yes, they are still trying to get an account but now they are being unobtrusive and non-threatening.

As an officer, your thoughts may purely surround the contents of the bag. If the detainee does not really appear to present a serious and immediate threat, then could you put the bag to one side until you ascertain their emotional status?

Joseph is 16 years old, 5 feet tall and weighs 8 stone. He doesn't initially fit the criteria as a dangerous offender. Handled correctly, he will not become so anxious that he reacts as he did in the scenario.

Using my advice, Joseph will calm sufficiently to shake his head to the officer's repeated question:

'Are you okay?'

Then he will say:

'No, the big boys were trying to get my books.'

The officer replies, 'I am here now and I will protect you, okay?'

Joseph nods.

'Can you show me your books please?' the officer asks.

Joseph thinks about this and slowly nods but does not seem to want to open the rucksack. Seeing this the officer reassesses their request:

'Do you want to open your rucksack on that bench where it is safe?'

Joseph nods more quickly this time. Removing him to a space where the officer has indicated it is 'safe' could be the all-important concept which up until now has eluded Joseph.

We know the bench isn't really a safe place but the officer has made it so simply by saying it is. Remember that autism has numerous layers of anxiety; remove them and you may receive engagement.

At no point has the officer needed to go 'hands on'. By using alternate strategies they have circumnavigated the need to do this. That is all this book is designed to do: give you advice to prevent it being necessary.

Stop and search/account are valuable provisions that, used correctly, can ensure public safety and confidence. Used badly they can result in unnecessary interactions with autistic people.

THINK. Is this person autistic?

Hands on or not?

It is a natural human reaction to assist others in need. Being a police officer, I would like to think that you would want to help everybody that you met, that you joined to do just that. So, when you see a person who looks like they are in trouble or upset, your instincts are going to kick in and you will go charging in like the proverbial knight in shining armour (or body armour these days).

STOP.

The person who you think may at first be in need of help may want the exact opposite. That person may be autistic and would like to be left alone. The example below highlights this point and will show how being a little 'gung ho' may result in unwanted interaction.

Having been trained to use all of the personal protection equipment on your utility belt, the first thing you are going to want to do under pressure is use it. This understandable reaction has been drummed into you for hours on end in a stuffy gymnasium. It is primarily for your own safety and secondly for the safety of those around you.

However, standing back and reassessing the person you have in front of you for even a few brief seconds could be all the time required to realise that the person is autistic.

Using the mantra STOP, LOOK, LISTEN, THINK you will then start to open the neural pathways to clear thinking. There is no need to charge into anything unless you absolutely have to. If all you remember on the street from this book is:

STOP! Is it autism?

there is a much greater chance of the whole picture becoming more clear and there being a positive outcome for everyone.

Once you have decided to touch the individual and go 'hands on' it places you in a precarious position from which stepping back is highly unlikely (although it can be done). Your touch can feel like extreme pain to the individual, making them react violently. This will cause you to grip tighter in order to secure the hold, which in turn makes them struggle more. It is an age-old circle that becomes ever harder to break free from. The likelihood of just letting go and allowing someone you have grappled with loose is unthinkable.

People with autism report that being unexpectedly touched is akin to a burning sensation or electric shock. I cannot overemphasise the seriousness of grabbing hold of someone with autism. What is taught as a simple restraint technique in the gym could be agony for the detained individual. Be sure that you are absolutely certain that you are ready to arrest, as it is almost a given that you are going to end up detaining this person.

In the next example, I have started to introduce other factors that will impact on your interactions with an autistic person.

Read it and see if you would do anything different from the start; with the all of this new knowledge you have gained so far, certain things should jump out as incorrect 'officer' behaviour. I will debrief it as before at the end.

EXAMPLE 5

An adult male is sitting slumped against the wall in a bus shelter. Someone has noticed he has been there for over an hour without moving and called the police. Upon arrival the officer sees an adult male dressed in a hooded top which has been pulled up and over, covering the top half of his face. He is wearing jeans and trainers and is grasping a carrier bag in his lap. The officer pulls alongside, lowers their window and shouts to the male, 'Aye up, mate, you alright?'

They receive no response. Fearing the male may be deceased, they exit the car and approach them.

Since arriving, they have not received any further information about the male and the caller has since left. As the officer slowly approaches, the male grunts and smiles. The officer is quietly grateful that they no longer have to deal with a sudden death. Feeling more confident, they call out again, 'Hey, mate, you okay?'

The male does not respond to their calls. As a passing thought, the officer notes how hot it is today and that the heavy clothing seems incongruous with the weather. Again they call out but receive no reply.

At this point all of their training is kicking in. They fiddle with their utility belt, subconsciously reassuring themselves the items are still there, selecting their weapon of choice. They reach out and place a hand on the shoulder of the male, shaking him.

His hood shoots back and he screams. His arms thrust towards the officer as he turns his head and body away. He then grabs the bag on his lap, clutching it to his chest, facing the far wall.

The officer steps back and draws their baton, giving a rehearsed instruction to the male: 'Get back!'

After a few seconds there is no reply; still holding their baton in a defensive posture, the officer gives a new command: 'Get down on the floor, get down!'

They are ignored as the male huddles away from the officer, cowering in the corner. The officer has called for assistance as this male is 6 feet tall and heavily built. Further commands are given to the male, all ignored.

Moving away towards their car, the officer waits for backup, keeping an eye on the male. When it arrives, there is a short, quiet discussion where the details of the interaction are briefly explained. A plan is quickly decided with silent gestures from the officers.

In a sudden movement, they grab the male without warning. Taking an arm each, they forcibly turn him towards them. The male struggles violently with an unbelievable strength. All three slide to the floor where the fight continues. The male continues to keep his hands underneath him whilst clinging onto his bag.

Finally after a hot, sweaty fight the officers subdue him, handcuffing him to the rear of his body, and eventually sit him up. He continues to struggle and scream, giving the officers no choice but to forcibly place him in the rear of the car, chuck his bag in after him and transport him to a custody unit nearby, restraining him all of the way.

Upon arrival he is so tired the officers are only able to present him to the sergeant if he is being supported each side. Now he is calm enough to search, his hood is pulled back fully revealing two dangling earbuds, attached to an MP3 device, still playing music. In his rear pocket is a small plastic pouch, which is tossed onto the counter for the sergeant to examine.

The pouch is clearly labelled and has an autism awareness card contained within it. The card gives all of his personal details and conditions. A conversation quickly takes place between the three officers.

Due to the lack of a real offence, the male, who they now know is called Sam, is uncuffed, de-arrested and sat down in a side room whilst his carer makes their way to the station. Contained in the 'suspicious' carrier bag is Sam's favourite soft toy, a cuddly bear named Albert.

DEBRIEF

As with all scenarios, they are clear in hindsight. No one likes to feel foolish. However, there are glaring errors in this example, which I will draw out to highlight some subtle signs to watch out for:

- Upon arrival Sam was dressed in clothing that the officer noted seemed too heavy for the warm day. If seen it should indicate you may be dealing with something out of the ordinary. Some autistic people like to habitually dress in the same clothes every day no matter what the weather. It makes them feel comfortable and at ease. A change of these can cause anxiety, which is always to be avoided.

- There was no response from Sam initially. This could have been for a number of reasons, but in this case, he was plugged into a music device. His world was completely enclosed. He was happy, sitting in his favourite place, the bus stop, listening to his favourite music.

- As far as Sam was concerned everyone in the area knows him and he is left alone to enjoy his hobby of bus watching. Just because there is no initial response, take time to reassess the situation. Although the male's hood was up, maybe sounds could be heard closer up? In this case they were on a busy road and the background noise could have masked the music, but that might not be the case every time.

- As the officer approached Sam, they saw him grunt and smile. This smile indicated the male was happy - benign - which is always a good base to start from. So perhaps attempting to attract their attention by a light tap and backing off would have been appropriate?

- Or perhaps even tapping a baton on the floor or bench that Sam was sat on could have attracted his attention? I put money on it that it would have. Although the tap/noise may have caused alarm, that would have been better than the end result.

- Touching Sam's arm got an unwanted response; he threw his long arms out in a defensive move but then immediately hid away from the officer in a huddle. This may indicate fear, possibly panic if the bag contained contraband or even a weapon.

- These are two completely separate avenues that the lone officer must explore within seconds. The heat of the situation is rising and clear decisions are hard to make. This is where the right training and input from an autism expert can be invaluable.

- If the officer has been taught about the subtleties of autism, they may have just stepped back and reassessed before they pressed the button for assistance or drew a defensive item.

- STOP, THINK, LOOK.

- If someone has not come out of their huddle after several seconds, not even to check if the officer is still there, then perhaps they do not want to or cannot. In these vital few seconds the officer can reassess; the person could even calm enough to unfold and engage.

- With the presence of another officer they are now in an even stronger position to communicate with Sam. By simply going 'hands on' they are circumnavigating all of the more logical steps. Now there are two sets of eyes with which to observe and more than enough safety equipment to defend themselves. So in these circumstances the whole approach could have been restarted, which in this case could have prevented the arrest.

- Whilst one officer is keeping watch on Sam, the other could have been making a call to control to see if there are any previous jobs about him or the bus stop. Speaking to anyone in the area could also reveal information to assist you. Explore all options possible before arrest.

- Once the officers had gone hands on, they destroyed any chance of a peaceful conclusion. Some people will automatically resist but a person like Sam could find the restraint so painful he will fight as hard as possible to break free.

- Another area of danger for Sam was the transportation to custody. Being held down or at a distance in the back of a car could potentially be life threatening, just one example being that restriction of movement can bring on an epileptic seizure. When dealing with autistic people always assume there are underlying medical issues; prevention is far better than cure in these circumstances.

- There are many strategies that could have been used in this scenario; however the ones I have chosen should be used as a starting block along with the rest of the book.

- At no time should you place yourself in danger when dealing with someone you do not know, even if you suspect they have autism. Your safety is paramount; however so is theirs.

- Do not *REACT* and *REGRET*. You *always* have the option to withdraw and reassess. Not many bobbies will use it, but it is better to look foolish than to face a discipline enquiry.

Now you have seen what can happen when you 'go hands on', I will explain further how the officers could have used more suitable strategies.

The individual is sat, back against a wall with a hoody pulled up over their head, arms wrapped tightly around their body. An initial shout, enquiring about their welfare, receives no response. There are now several options, perhaps another call of 'Are you okay?' could be made. You could try moving closer then try again, perhaps even going right up to them, kneeling to one side (ensuring your own safety) and saying, 'Hi, I am a police officer/paramedic/enforcement officer...are you okay?' in the initial instance.

If you receive a response of, 'Go away!' then consider backing off a few feet. It may just be an automatic response, used many times with local bullies with no malice intended towards you. At least you have made contact and can move on to the next stage.

If there is no response but you can tell from their movements that the individual is breathing, another option, as I have already mentioned, could be a tap of a baton near to them to attract their attention. Maybe you could try saying, 'I am just going to touch your arm to see if you are well...okay?' By doing this, you are giving them chance to process and react.

Wait for a response. It may feel like an eternity to wait up to ten seconds but you may find this has given the individual enough time to process what you are going to do.

Being in such close proximity you must be guided by personal safety at all times. Vigilance is paramount, however at this point the safety of the individual is also important and if no response has been obtained then other impact factors must be considered, such as an illness or medical condition – diabetes for example – as well as intoxication through drink or drugs.

Tell them again you are going to touch them: 'Hi, I am going to touch your arm now.'

As your hand touches the individual's arm they might flinch violently, moving away and swearing. This is not necessarily a bad thing: it shows they are alive and responsive.

Now, STOP. THINK. Are they autistic?

Back off if required and repeat all of the above processes.

At every stage, hopefully information is being fed to you via radio or phone and intelligence about the individual should be coming through to inform The National Decision Model (NDM) in your mind. All of this can take only a matter of seconds and doesn't have to last all day. As with any technique, once practised this will become second nature. The more often it is done, the more efficient the process will be. This system can work with anyone and any situation; it is completely transportable. Dealing with anyone you encounter in this way can be just as beneficial. All it comes down to is respect for the other person, which surely can be only a good thing.

As with any scenario, I have placed an autistic person at the centre. I am not naïve enough to think that every male slumped in a bus stop is autistic. If you truly feel after using the first seven of the Golden Rules that the person in front of you is not autistic but dangerous, then by all means revert to your training and deal with them in the way you see fit. This book is designed to give you options and even if the individual is intoxicated and volatile, my advice still stands: STOP, THINK, ASSESS.

If you have repeated all of the stages above and are still not receiving any reply then there are few options left than to go hands on and actually touch the person. Touching someone is an intimate thing; invading their personal space is normally done without thinking. To an autistic person this can be the most intrusive thing anyone can do. Advice about how you go about this will be down to your personality, training and previous experience amongst others. I will not dictate a manner in which you do this, as advising a firm or a light touch could be completely inappropriate to the person in front of you.

Whatever your route, be decisive and make a plan but be willing to change it if it all goes wrong. No one is perfect and genuine mistakes are made. In my experience a confident manner is always best, not arrogant: confident, respectful and adaptable. Mercurial decision making is the way to navigate autism; that is, being flexible and not afraid to admit error. If you don't know, say, ask. Not many in the autistic world have ever complained about an officer who has stuck their hands up and said they don't know. It is a good adage for life, and even better in autism circles.

Restraint and transportation

The dangers surrounding this are real and require clear explanation. I will set out what can be awaiting you, should you find yourself suddenly gripping an autistic person tightly, and what to do and what not to do under *any* circumstance.

At this point all of the niceties will have dissipated, as in the heat of the moment the last thing you will be concerned about is conversational pleasantries. Your primary aim is to transport a detainee as quickly as possible with the least hassle.

If the autistic person has reacted badly to being touched, then it may be that the 'hands-on' scenario has stepped up a level and full-on restraint has been necessary. Other factors may now be impacting on the autistic person too. Intoxicants or mental health issues could very well be making them violent. At this point, it is all too easy to simply bundle them into a waiting vehicle and whisk them off to custody...

STOP.

In the rear of the car or carrier, there is an even higher chance of a life-threatening incident occurring. I include positional asphyxia (PA) when speaking about a person who is face down on the floor. Regardless of whether an autistic person has any physical differences (this is sometimes dwelt on far too heavily in my opinion), keep an extra vigilant eye on them if you have the slightest suspicion you may be dealing with *any* neurodiverse person. Keep the airways open at all times and lie them on their side at the very least. Your force should have provided training on this subject; if not then seek professional medical advice on the matter.

Remember, the person you have in your immediate custody is also in your *care*. If the person you are dealing with is autistic, then they have a statistically higher liklihood of having a co-morbid illness, such as a heart condition, asthma or epilepsy. The mere fact they are being restrained/cuffed/confined in the vehicle could be enough to trigger a seizure. This is applicable for any detainee and of course PACE clearly sets out guidelines for dealing with people after arrest so I will not linger on it but feel obliged to highlight that autistic people should be afforded an extra degree of caution.

Talk to the autistic person: reassure them you are there to help, tell them where they are going and what will happen to them when they get there. This is always assuming they are not offering violence to you. If the journey is long, the detainee may start to calm down, enabling dialogue to recommence. This does not always happen but at any point there is still an opportunity to start talking once again. Switch off the two-tones if safe to do so; these can be painful and disturbing to the person.

Once you have reached the rear yard of the designated custody block, and *before* entering the building, you may wish to consider removing the handcuffs or repositioning them from the rear to the front. This is of course only applicable if the person has calmed sufficiently and you have first searched them for weapons or other hazardous articles. Waiting in the holding area can be a lengthy process in a busy suite and an uncomfortable wait for all concerned.

A custody suite is an extremely frightening place for any vulnerable person. All sorts of hell will be pictured in their head. Don't forget this may be the very first time they have ever met an officer, let alone been arrested. The officer feels safe there; the same cannot be said for the terrified detained person.

Taking a few seconds to explain to them that they are going to be treated with respect and dignity in exchange for compliance may focus their mind. This is not to say that you are demanding absolute supplication, getting them to beg for mercy. Stating that they will be treated fairly if they do not shout, swear or offer violence when presented to the sergeant is a clear and unambiguous request.

Call ahead and inform the block that you are bringing in someone with autism and request that you are allowed straight in if possible. Depending on how busy they are the sergeant should grant your request. It will not be popular with those around you, but you will be abiding by the rules in this book to afford the autistic person as much assistance as possible. It will also be in the sergeant's best interests to book in the calmest person they can; waiting is just going to exacerbate the situation. Anything that can be done to reduce anxiety and stress must be considered.

One for the 'thought locker'

Whilst researching this book I have read so many disturbing examples of police behaviour worldwide when dealing with autism, that I feel obliged to include the following:

Being a police officer brings many wonderful attributes to the table when dealing with autistic people. You are fastidious, decisive and well trained in the application of the law. You can be relied upon to protect the innocent and have a respected place in society.

At the same time, you also have the power to detain, restrain and incapacitate those very individuals that you are paid to safeguard.

I have mentioned previously that you have a utility belt with several defensive options upon it. If you have to use one, please make it the last resort. Far too many vulnerable people have been seriously hurt or even died because of the use of one of these weapons. I know from bitter experience that there are times when you have no option but to use them and they have saved my life in the process. However I have also witnessed unnecessary use of them.

As I have outlined before, autistic people can have co-morbid conditions which will be seriously affected by your use of, for example, a TASER™. If you are a firearms officer then your mere presence at an incident would indicate that it has escalated to a much more serious level and beyond the remit of this book.

Striking an autistic person with a baton, drive-stunning them or using rigid cuffs to achieve compliance has been discussed at length in several journals around the world and I do not wish to glorify what they seem to suggest are 'acceptable' techniques to gain the upper hand.

If the person with autism is not being cooperative, STOP. THINK. *Why?*

Why are they not doing what I want them to?

Why are they standing there rocking from side to side, clicking their fingers?

What am I *not* doing to aid their communication?

In pulling a weapon from your belt and holding it, you will no doubt feel much safer and you have been told time after time that they are there to protect *you*, but who is protecting *them*? If they are barely aggressive and offering little or no violence then STOP, STEP BACK and ASSESS.

Is your use of this piece of metal or plastic going to damage the autistic person?

What have they done, really? Is your hand on that particular piece of equipment simply because you want it or is it necessary? Once you have gone to the point of using it, you are in a vicious circle and stepping back from a strike or discharge is not going to happen.

The person you are opposite may be so scared that they are physically unable to move, let alone speak. The only thing they may be doing at that moment is soiling themselves, as that is an unconscious reaction to *your* direct aggression.

The autistic person is *not* an animal. They are a human being. Treat them as such. The use of your equipment must be the final resort, after *everything* else has been tried and failed. Far too many officers use it as a first step.

In using my Golden Rules, you may not have to do any of that. You could get compliance and a cooperative person with simple courtesy.

Try it first, *then* resort to more extreme techniques.

Please do not lie in the still of the night, regretting something you could have so easily avoided by using this book as your guide.

In the next example I will show you how a change in approach will prevent any need for an officer to regret their actions.

EXAMPLE 6

An officer is on patrol when they are called to a report of an assault, shoplifting and criminal damage. As the officer makes it to the area a better description of the offender comes in as well as an approximate location. The officer sees a male fitting the description sitting on a bench in a patch of grass around the corner from the shop. They stop and approach the male. As they get closer, they can see him rocking back and forth and gripping something in his outstretched left hand. This unnerves the officer, who calls out to the male, 'You alright, mate?'

No reply. He just keeps staring into space and rocking.

The officer comes within ten feet of the male who he can hear wailing at a very high pitch. 'Mate? You alright, mate?'

The sausage roll in his hand is squeezed tightly, squirting tomato sauce all over the floor. The noise continues.

There is something not right about this guy but the officer has the correct person; he fits the description and he has the stolen item on him. The officer has received no autism training and has not read this book. They approach the male, wave a hand in front of his face and when no reply is received, grabs the male by the shoulder and shakes him.

The male screams and barges past the officer, knocking them aside.

The officer is alarmed at this behaviour and the sudden assault. They pursue the male, who is not quick on his feet and is soon caught. The officer rugby tackles the male to the floor where a struggle ensues. The male is quickly overpowered, arrested and cuffed to the rear still holding the sausage roll. The officer informs control they have one male under arrest and are making for custody with the offender on board.

The male does nothing but scream all the way to custody, really annoying the officer, who is hot, sweaty and covered in tomato sauce. At custody, they present the male, who does not engage at all but offers no further violence. The custody sergeant starts the procedure but receives a phone call almost immediately. They look at the detained person (DP) then the officer and rings off. 'That was the control room. It appears that this male is well known to the shop, he lives just around the corner. He has autism and the store alarm went off, causing him to bolt from the shop. The call was to locate him, there have been no complaints made at all. The doors are okay, the injured man knows the male's dad and has in fact paid for the property taken.'

'Aw, sorry, sarg... I didn't know.'

Wrong person to apologise to.

DEBRIEF

Let me rewind.

Having learned the Golden Rules, it is now easy to see where the mistakes were made. As I have said previously, this is not a stick to beat anyone with; I am simply hoping to jog memories and show best practice. This scenario could have been so easily dealt with in a different way. I will break it down into sections to show how many layers this has:

This is how the call initially came into control on the nines (999 system):

'We have just had Martin in here, the alarm went off and he panicked, running out with a sausage roll that he hadn't paid for and he pushed old Mr Edston and cut his head, he's very shaken and the doors don't open as quick as they should and Martin banged into them and now they are jammed and we can't get out after him. Can you send someone quick to find him, please? It's not right, he's autistic, you have to find him.'

Are there any offences? Yes.

Is the offender still on the premises? No.

Does anyone require ambulance services? Injured but refused aid.

Is the offender known? Yes. Martin. Description obtained.

Where are they? In the close-by area.

Patrols nearby? Yes. Alpha 18 is in location. Dispatch.

What information is the patrol initially given? They are told there have been three offences, given a quick rundown of them and a description of the offender.

SORRY Martin.

Why was the patrol not told he was autistic? This is a massive game leveller. The woman in the shop is not telling the call handler Martin is autistic because she is disgusted by it; she is worried and quite rightly so. They all know him and can see he is extremely vulnerable due to the incident.

How long have they known him? Well, Mr Edston has known him all his life as he went to school with his dad and he is in his 60s. Martin is a part of the community and usually protected by them. The only reason the call to the police was made was because the doors were stuck and they couldn't get out fast enough to find him and see if he was okay.

What is recorded and how it is written goes a long way in directing how the job is handled.

Let's rewrite this first section with the Golden Rules in place and the call handler trained in autism:

When they heard the word autism, that jumped out at them. Martin is in a shop where he has always gone since he was little; he feels comfortable and safe there. The people in the shop know him well. So why has he suddenly panicked? This would be a good line of thought from the call handler. This information will lead to the job being put on to the system correctly, so the dispatcher (if different) sees it.

Martin panicked because someone knocked over a box in the storeroom setting off the alarm. Why is this important?

Being autism aware, the call taker knows that sudden loud noises can be very upsetting for autistic people. All other priorities are immediately disregarded and exit is the only option, to get as far away from the noise as possible.

So Martin's reaction is now understandable.

As Martin tried to leave the store he did not see anything else apart from the doors. Mr Edston was walking up the aisle to say hello to Martin as he has known him since birth. He sees him panicking and tries to step back knowing Martin is going to run. It is too late and he barges past Mr Edston, who is only concerned about him. There is no assault here - there never was and the lady from the shop makes this clear.

SORRY Martin.

The doors open inwards, but as Martin charges into them, in blind fear, he pushes them, popping the hinges, which swing back and stick. They are old metal doors that regularly jam on the carpet. Replacements are expensive and a good shove usually fixes them. There is no criminal damage here. Martin never intended to cause damage to anything and wasn't being reckless.

SORRY Martin.

The call taker asks, 'How is Martin usually?' They are told he has always been calm, he is 30 years old, he chats but not too much and is usually polite. He comes in every day to buy a sausage roll, a bag of crisps and a can of pop and has done for longer than anyone can remember. He is a lovely lad.

Immediately that one question has opened up a flood of answers. It is not a series of offences the police are investigating; it is a vulnerable person with autism called Martin. By using his name you are personalising the situation. It no longer is a thief in a shop; it becomes someone who is part of the local community, a friend to everyone.

SORRY Martin.

Let's see how it now sounds with the Golden Rules running in the background:

'Alpha 18 receiving?...

Alpha 18 not committed in Broad Street...

> Thank you 18, we have just had a call from Alf's shop on Main Road, a local lad with autism called Martin has been scared by the shop alarm and has run off with some goods from there, he accidently knocked someone over and jammed the doors but there are no complaints. There is concern for his safety, can you attend the area and await update please?...
>
> Yes, no problems book me to it...'

See how changing the description of the incident has put it in the officer's mind? He is no longer just an offender with stolen goods who has assaulted someone and damaged the doors; he is a *vulnerable* person with autism.

Whilst the officer is looking for Martin, the call taker can be asking more questions in the background. What is his full name? Where does he live? Does he have a carer? Is there a phone number for them? Mr Edston, who is sitting down in the storeroom with a cup of tea, might know.

A call to Martin's carer reveals even more. Is he ever violent? No. Does he speak freely? Yes, when not stressed. Are there any other triggers that make him distressed? Yes, touching him makes him scream. Is he on any medication? Yes, he has a heart condition and asthma; any extreme stress or blows to the chest are potentially life threatening.

This last one is a massive game changer. Many autistic people have other physical conditions (called co-morbid) which impact on their daily lives. Heart conditions, breathing difficulties and eye problems are just a few. The officer went to deal with Martin and ended up taking him to the floor and then restraining him. Both of these could have caused serious if not life-threatening injuries.

SORRY Martin.

So, the officer is now fully briefed as to Martin's background. Let's raise the bar slightly and say that although not trained in autism, they have done an online module that gave them a brief overview of the condition. They completed it only a few days ago and it is still fairly new and bouncing around their head.

(The use of online modules is hotly debated in the training arena. Whatever your opinion on them, I always advocate the use of quality training from autistic trainers who are present to answer any questions that arise. The benefits of someone with real-life experience giving a talk on a subject far outweighs anything a computer program can deliver. The use of online training is something that your own force will ultimately decide.)

The officer vaguely remembers something about not shouting at autistic people and something else. What was it? Possibly flapping their hands, they think. Seeing Martin, they stop the car and walk towards him, their radio blaring away on their chest. As they approach, they call out, 'You okay, mate?' They receive no reply, so walk closer. They have forgotten the first rule already; however all is not lost.

Control call them up and tell them everything they have just learned from Martin's carer. Now, they remember the part about being calm; it comes back to the officer just in time. They stop and turn their radio down to a more appropriate level. 'Martin? Are you okay, Martin?' they ask in a softer tone, 6 feet away. They can see the sausage roll and tomato sauce, but this time it is only an indication that it is the right person and that they are upset.

The officer moves close enough to touch Martin and reaches out but suddenly remembers the invaluable advice from control and immediately withdraws their hand. They ask again and Martin seems to be rocking less and the high-pitched noise lessens.

The officer kneels and looks up at Martin. 'Can you hear me, Martin?' Slowly his eyes slide down to look at the officer but are glazed. 'It's okay, Martin, your dad is coming, he'll be here soon, it's all going to be okay.'

The noise stops.

Martin's dad comes running towards them, panting and sweating. 'Don't touch him, officer!' he manages to say.

The officer stands and backs off. 'It's okay, sir, control told me not to. I have just been making sure Martin was okay, haven't I, Martin?'

Martin stands, drops the sausage roll and runs to his dad, hugging him. His dad hugs him back and says to the officer, 'Thank you so much, the last time he ran off, the police found him and it went very badly.'

'That's okay, sir, we are here to help. I am going to go to Alf's and see what happened there. Do you need a lift?'

'No thank you officer, we'll walk. Martin doesn't like cars much. If there's any damage, I'll pay for it. I'm just glad Martin is okay.'

'Me too, sir. Goodbye then...bye, Martin'.

There is no need to say sorry now.

All it took was the time for dad to get the call and make his way around to where Martin and the officer were. Just a few simple, informed questions and probing from the control room staff was all it took to save what could have been a very nasty incident for the officer and force at large.

If you are control room staff, remember that what you record will determine what happens next down the line. Ask all the questions you can from the informant. If autism is mentioned, record it. Ask for details of a carer or at least someone who knows the person. Direct the patrols to the best result. Give them all of the information you have and request feedback. Get to know what is happening and if you think someone is not sticking to the Golden Rules, then you or the duty officer (or whoever is in charge) make a record of what they do and try to steer them back on track.

As the officer on the street, if you are not receiving enough information then ask for more. If you suspect autism or are told, then follow the rules and direct the situation in the correct way. Ultimately it is your job on the line. Following the advice in this book can save it. The Golden Rules are simple, almost 'bobby proof', although very little is. Read the rules, ask questions and do not assume anything.

Please: Only go hands on if you really, really, really have to.

Carer assistance

It could be that you are called to a report of a violent disturbance in a public carpark or even at someone's home. When attending and you see someone holding the arm of a much younger individual who is shouting or screaming, STOP. THINK AUTISM.

This may be a parent or carer struggling to hold onto an autistic person.

Instead of rushing up and wrenching their grip off the younger individual, perhaps approach them and ask if you can help. It may look like an assault at first but you will soon see that there is no violence involved, and it is a restraining technique instead. You will be experienced enough to see the difference between the two and I will not dwell on how you can tell one from the other.

Something may have disturbed or upset the autistic person and their carer is doing their best to get them into the car. This is difficult enough without someone else interfering. They will have practised countless techniques over the years and fine-tuned them to reach this point. If you go barging in and start to boss everyone around, this will only cause more problems.

Letting go of the autistic individual is the last thing the carer wants to do, as they may have coerced them all the way back to the car over the last hour or so. Releasing them could start the process all over again. As previously explained, I do not want you to go hands on unless absolutely necessary; this situation is definitely included.

You could be a great help: seeing you may calm the individual down by being fearful of you. This could edge them into the car without any further assistance. Once again, it may not and all hell may break loose. It can only go better if you are willing to listen to the carer's pleas. Watch what they say and see if you can help rather than hinder.

The carer is going to be extremely embarrassed to have you there. I am willing to bet they are not the ones who have called you. This will probably be the ever-so-helpful 'bystander' who has stood and watched the carer struggle with the autistic person and instead of helping out, much prefers to stand in judgement and call on the police to step in. All the carer will want to do is get the individual in the car and get them home as they know this situation is upsetting them.

Try to see it from their point of view.

Instead of running up and shouting, 'Hey now, let's have less of that', grabbing hold of the autistic person and making it worse, try walking up and asking from a few feet away, 'Can I be of assistance?'

If you receive a quick, 'No thank you, officer, everything is fine, we just need to get in the car that's all', don't take this as a dismissive insult. STOP. THINK AUTISM.

You could even ask, 'Are they autistic?' Again, you may not receive a positive answer or one at all, but you might get a raised eyebrow. Take this as a silent affirmation and use the Golden Rules to assist the carer and autistic person. Try putting your palms out and stepping back, saying, 'It's okay, I understand. I will not become involved unless you want me to but I am going to back off and observe just in case'.

The carer may well be sweating profusely, tired, upset and now mightily embarrassed. Having a screaming child/adult bringing reproachful looks from all around is bad enough but, now the police have arrived it just makes everything ten times worse.

By all means, stay and observe, maybe even back off a bit more, speak to the informant if you wish, update control and keep watching but, do not be judgemental. Look at everything that is going on around you. Does the autistic person look injured or in need of medical help? If not then they should be okay. The call will always be yours and if you feel that you need to step in to assist or even arrest then do so. My advice aims simply to give you more options.

If you arrive at the home address (H/A) of the autistic person and a similar scenario is occurring inside the house then treat it in the same manner as I have already described. In the case of being at home, the autistic person may well be trying to get out or everything around them feels overwhelming. For the carer it may well be another difficult day. STOP. THINK AUTISM. Do not go charging in; give the situation a thorough examination before you decide on what to do. Give the carer the benefit of the doubt; what you first see may not be how it really is.

A room in disarray and people still in their pyjamas in the middle of the day is not automatically a sign of neglect. After a sleepless night, they may have only just got up. Autistic people sometimes have extremely disrupted sleep patterns; some may not sleep very much at all. So it is the carer who must try to survive on two hours sleep (often still disturbed) in any 24 hours.

Talk to the carers and the autistic people; see what really is occurring and how their lives could be improved. If eventually all is well, ask yourself, 'What can I do to help?'

Try to leave their home in a positive mood or even frame of mind. By talking to everyone in that house, you could leave them feeling a tiny bit more assured they can trust the police and not be terrified of them.

The 'runner'

Before long you are going to be called to a missing person or 'mis-per'. They may be a first time report or a persistent mis-per or 'runner'. This term has long been used to describe someone (usually a juvenile) who runs as soon as they see a police uniform. The usual connotation is linked to criminal activity and the police parlance will drift across the radio airwaves when in pursuit of a suspect: 'I have a runner here.'

The possible reasons causing the mis-per to go in the first place are far too many to list. Each case will be different to the last. Autistic people (including children) may want to see something that has just taken their eye or they may like the feel of freedom in a local park. It will sometimes be quite innocuous and very little thought will have gone into the act. It may be the result that has driven their absence and no planning was involved in reaching it. They also may have no conception of being lost; in their mind they are exactly where they want to be, so why would that be a worry? This can be a problem for you when it comes to trying to return them home: that's not where they want to be.

In other cases of autism and particularly ADHD, the hyperactivity and impulsivity of the autistic person can cause them to become embroiled with petty or low-level crime. This in turn can result in a desire to avoid the law at all costs and a lot of work has been put in by officers around the country to engage with these people to try to turn their offending around.

The use of computer systems to record vast data files on missing persons has contributed to a much better cohesion of intelligence but the sheer size of the information contained in these systems does seem to overwhelm you when scrolling back through the previous entries on recurrent individuals. However, gathering as much information as you can on the background of the mis-per will pay dividends.

If you are called to an autistic mis-per, pause for a moment to think: why have they done this? A lot of families have little real control over the containment of an autistic person. Barring the windows and doors can be done (and in some cases are), but these are temporary measures and do not stop the urge in the runner.

However, if you attend an autistic home and see these seemingly barbaric steps to prevent an episode, please stand back and remember my words: to some families, a runner is a way of life for them, something that started in childhood and has simply continued. They may not have had any support and tried their best to avoid constant criticism from many different services including the police.

When you next ask, 'What are you doing to stop them from becoming missing?' take a moment to consider how living with the stress of autism 24 hours a day can be impacting on the mental health of the carers. Instead, think, 'What can I do to help these people?'

Having been despatched to a runner, how do you deal with them when they see you and run? It is a really annoying situation, when you seem to get close enough to engage with the person, only to find they leg it away before you can speak to them. The information you have obtained from the mis-per system, or better still first hand from the carers, should have given you the heads-up about the autistic person and what you can do help the situation.

One example I have is so simple it seems ludicrous.

EXAMPLE 7

Having been told a missing 11-year-old with autism had been sighted in a park, I attended with a colleague as we were the area car for the day. The description was spot on and soon enough we saw the lad by the swings. At this point he had been missing for several hours and there were genuine concerns for his safety.

Exiting the car we casually walked up to him and upon seeing us he bolted for the far end of the park. To say he was quick is an understatement; he was like a whippet. I can take no credit for the next events. My colleague (younger and far fitter than me) took off after him. Halfway across the grass he threw off his reflective coat but continued after the lad calling his name. Why had he done this? Even I was puzzled. Was he just too hot?

Eventually, after collecting his jacket I received a radio message that he was with the lad and all was well. They were coming back to the car but could I also remove my traffic jacket? Confused I did as instructed and was greeted by a shy but smiling young man called Adrian and a flushed-faced colleague.

Once Adrian was safely back with his grateful family, I had to ask, 'What was the jacket thing all about?'

This is what my colleague said: 'I remember this lad. I used to work on the patch and recall something his mum had told the local lads. She said he had a fear of yellow jackets. He associated it with capture and return to the house. If anyone ever went near him in one he would bolt, so I suddenly remembered and chucked it off. Once I was in black, I could call out to him and he stopped. I was terrified he would get to the railway line at the bottom of the bank before I got to him.'

It was that simple. This officer's hidden memory of Adrian possibly could have saved his life; his quick thinking and positive action stopped the running. Was the officer autism trained? Back then, no. It was long before I was diagnosed, so even I had little knowledge of it, but I recognised his thought pattern perfectly.

This example has stuck with me for well over twenty years. Something easy, linked with a genuine wish to help gave an immediate result. This is what I am advocating throughout this book. You don't need to be an expert, just willing to help. My colleague didn't even consider autism when they acted. It wasn't a conscious thought, they just acted correctly. You can do that, without any training and probably do, every day. What this book is intended to do is give you information and allow you to choose what suits you best.

With most runners, there will be a reason they are where you find them. Try to discover from other sources what it is. If they immediately run again upon seeing you, remain calm, focus and THINK AUTISM. What can *you* do to help *them*?

If you can get close enough to speak to them, use reassurance; tell them you are there to help. This may seem a silly instruction, but it is amazing how many bobbies don't do it. They forget that the person is as frightened as a cornered bunny. They may be thinking of when they are taken home again and the retribution. Whatever it is, you can help allay those fears. Keep in view that they may have been (mis)handled dozens of times by various services and have no wish to engage with yet another nasty person in uniform.

Use the Golden Rules. Keep calm and as before *do not* go hands on unless you must.

When you return them to their home (care or family) don't just dump them and walk off, job done. Spend some time with them and try (if they will let you – it isn't always the case) to see what you can do to help the situation. If there is anything, it may start to prevent them running again. This is a good thing, for them and you. The less time you have to spend pursuing runners, the more you can spend visiting local autistic establishments and publicly engaging with them; this too can only be for the good of everyone.

If it has sadly reached the point where you are transporting them to custody then try to keep calm and use the information in the next section to assist the autistic person you have now detained.

In the custody block

Now we are entering the custody block, it is essential that you are familiar with PACE:

The Police and Criminal Evidence Act 1984

CODE C Revised Code of Practice for the detention, treatment and questioning of persons by Police Officers

The Code of Practice Part C – Detention was updated July 2018 and although updates are common, these for 2018 were brought in to protect vulnerable people and juveniles.

The government has published the reasons behind the changes:

The revisions to Code C introduce a new definition of 'vulnerable' to describe a person for whom an appropriate adult must be called, supported by a new requirement for proactive steps to identify and record factors which indicate that a suspect may require help and support from an appropriate adult and provisions which update the role description of the appropriate adult and who may or may not act in this capacity. The requirement to identify factors that indicate vulnerability is also extended to juveniles for whom an appropriate adult must always be called.

Please note the use of the word 'must' in line two. This is a new diversion away from the ambiguous, 'should'. The more detailed explanations are below and will prove interesting to custody staff.

Locating a copy of Code C has always been difficult enough in any custody unit; the most recent edition is nigh-on impossible and as such I have included the excerpts for ease of reference below. I have copied the relevant sections that are most pertinent for you. They have been taken from source and not adjusted in any way. They are not onerous reading but their style of writing can seem heavy going. I will interpret them as we go along, to show you how their use is required by law and must be adhered to at all times and is not simply 'optional' when in custody.

The most important one for any booking-in process is:

1.4 If at any time an officer has any reason to suspect that a person of any age may be vulnerable (see paragraph 1.13(d)), in the absence of clear evidence to dispel that suspicion, that person shall be treated as such for the purposes of this Code.

The code goes onto explain how the custody officer shall cause enquiries to be made into the background of the detainee. A full explanation can be found in the codes.

My advice is: when booking anyone in always err on the side of caution and if you have any suspicions then treat the detainee as vulnerable.

1.13(d) 'vulnerable' applies to any person who, because of a mental health condition or mental disorder (see Notes 1G and 1GB):

  i. may have difficulty understanding or communicating effectively about the full implications for them of any procedures and processes connected with:

- *their arrest and detention; or (as the case may be)*

- *their voluntary attendance at a police station or their presence elsewhere (see paragraph 3.21), for the purpose of a voluntary interview; and*

- *the exercise of their rights and entitlements.*

  ii. does not appear to understand the significance of what they are told, of questions they are asked or of their replies:

  iii. appears to be particularly prone to:

- *becoming confused and unclear about their position;*

- *providing unreliable, misleading or incriminating information without knowing or wishing to do so;*

- *accepting or acting on suggestions from others without consciously knowing or wishing to do so; or*

- *readily agreeing to suggestions or proposals without any protest or question.*

As can be seen, the person can be arrested or have arrived as a voluntary suspect to be interviewed. Be careful to treat an autistic person as vulnerable whether in or out of custody, during part of any investigation.

PACE continues to explain what exactly vulnerable means:

1G A person may be vulnerable as a result of a having a mental health condition or mental disorder. Similarly, simply because an individual does not have, or is not known to have, any such condition or disorder, does not mean that they are not vulnerable for the purposes of this Code. It is therefore important that the custody officer in the case of a detained person or the officer investigating the offence in the case of a person who has not been arrested or detained, as appropriate, considers on a case by case basis, whether any of the factors described in paragraph 1.13(d) might apply to the person in question. In doing so, the officer must take into account the particular circumstances of the individual and how the nature of the investigation might affect them and bear in mind that juveniles, by virtue of their age will always require an appropriate adult.

This section outlines the thought process when considering how you deal with detainees. Note that the new section clearly states that there does *not* have to be a condition present; the mere suspicion is sufficient. This is where this book will help you: follow my advice and treat *all* vulnerable people as autistic and it will benefit everyone.

Considering factors when dealing with vulnerable people:

1GA For the purposes of paragraph 1.4(a), examples of relevant information that may be available include:

- *the behaviour of the adult or juvenile;*

- *the mental health and capacity of the adult or juvenile;*

- *what the adult or juvenile says about themselves;*

- *information from relatives and friends of the adult or juvenile;*

- *information from police officers and staff and from police records;*

- *information from health and social care (including liaison and diversion services) and other professionals who know, or have had previous contact with, the individual and may be able to contribute to assessing their need for help and support from an 11 Codes of practice – Code C Detention, treatment and questioning of persons by police officers appropriate adult. This includes contacts and assessments arranged by the police or at the request of the individual or (as applicable) their appropriate adult or solicitor.*

These are relevant suggestions and align perfectly with the rules in this book.

Furthermore, the codes set out the need for appropriate adults (AAs) which I will cover shortly:

3.15 If the detainee is a juvenile or a vulnerable person, the custody officer must, as soon as practicable, ensure that:

- *the detainee is informed of the decision that an appropriate adult is required and the reason for that decision (see paragraph 3.5(c)(ii)) and;*

- *the detainee is advised: ~ of the duties of the appropriate adult as described in paragraph 1.7A; and ~ that they can consult privately with the appropriate adult at any time.*

- *the appropriate adult, who in the case of a juvenile may or may not be a person responsible for their welfare, as in paragraph 3.13, is informed of: ~ the grounds for their detention; ~ their whereabouts; and*

- *the attendance of the appropriate adult at the police station to see the detainee is secured.*

That is the PACE section set aside for a short while. I will return to it in subsequent sections but I will now resume with your arrival in the block.

If possible use a 'quiet' facility to book in the person with autism, away from others, where they can be shielded from other 'customers'. Be patient. Listen to their responses, demands and fears with an open mind. Also if a fire alarm test is due, explain this too. A sudden sound can completely disrupt their train of thought, missing vital information you could need.

When booking in watch for non-verbal communications (NVCs); a sudden drumming of fingers, tapping of a foot or a raised eyebrow can signal they are not divulging all they could to the question asked. Further investigation of these areas may lead to a truthful answer. Some people with autism do not wish to divulge their diagnosis as they are embarrassed or fearful of persecution. If the questions directly use the phrase 'autism or learning disability', they may feel more confident to talk about it.

If the detained person refuses to divulge their neurodiversity but it is already on the system, then allow them their privacy; don't challenge them by demanding it. Make a note on the system then put in all of the safety measures around them; an AA and alerting staff is a sufficient start.

In my own force I advocated for an extension to the risk assessment on the booking-in computer system. Several more questions were submitted for inclusion in the section relating to help with reading or writing. If the answer to any question was yes, was that due to dyslexia or even a lack of education?

In the mental health section, in addition to the usual questions, I inserted 'Do you have autism? If yes, what help do you need?' This question is different to stating that you know that they have autism; it gives the DP the opportunity to answer, rather than demanding it. The direct question did yield positive results and afterwards several detainees said they were grateful it had been asked.

These were just a few of the suggested changes. I found that they were a sound basis on which to start a direct investigation into a diagnosis or even suspected trait of neurodiversity. The more you can ascertain about a detained person the better, especially if it is autism; an early heads-up can be invaluable.

If your custody system already has this facility, then the chance of identifying autism will increase greatly. If not, it may be something that the force can add without too much disruption to the already overloaded system. If it is not possible to include them, then simply making note of these questions (possibly laminating them for everyone to use) and asking the DP if they have autism or co-morbid conditions will be sufficient. It is obtaining the answers that is the goal.

At the point when the offer of legal advice and having someone informed of their detention is reached, telling the autistic person that they will be reminded of their rights when their AA arrives can be another trigger for them to acknowledge their need for assistance. If no details of their carer are available from previous records then another suitable person must be sought. The final request from the DP for someone who can act for them may show them that hiding their neurodiversity is unnecessary. Keep reassuring them they will be treated with respect whilst they are in custody. The bottom line is clear: PACE dictates that if you receive information that they are vulnerable you must act. Their privacy will have to be put to one side in preference for adherence to the law.

Explaining to the autistic person that you are aware of their need for an AA can sometimes produce anger. They may state they are perfectly capable of looking after themselves and have no need of one. If they have had one previously in custody at *any* time whilst an adult then err on the side of caution and call in the assistance of a health care professional (HCP). You are not qualified to decide that they seem fine. Many have been criticised for doing exactly that.

The other group of people with autism is those who have not yet discovered they are autistic. These are the many who slip through the CJS until it is picked up either in prison or hospital. If you see something or feel that the person in front of you could be neurodiverse then treat them as such. Do not divulge your thoughts to them as they may find it offensive. You can call a HCP at any point and do not have to justify it. PACE dictates quite clearly on these matters, so seek advice, but put in place all of the measures I suggest in this book and you may find that the DP is less anxious whilst in your care.

At this point I want to mention 'easy read' documents. These simplified explanations assisted with pictures clearly set out a detainee's lawful entitlements. They were filtering through into many custody suites around the country whilst I was still in there. They have been championed by many of the charities around the country, specifically those working with learning disabilities and autism. Their introduction into the CJS has made an invaluable addition in explaining the extremely complex aspects of PACE, some of which even police officers struggle with. There should be no stigma in having easy read explanations clearly displayed around a custody suite as they can benefit an even larger section of society who ends up there, such as foreign nationals. I often used them whilst searching for the correct language when booking in an immigration matter as the pictures are self-explanatory.

If you do not have copies of the easy read version of rights and entitlements then a search online should furnish you with them. Also approach your local autism charities for further information and guidance on the incredible impact they have had in that arena. They will be only too happy to work with you and your force.

Searching can be another flash point: people in general do not like to be searched. It is an intrusion into their personal space. An autistic person is just the same. As mentioned previously, talk to the person, tell them what you are doing, why and what you want them to do. Be direct and polite, keep it simple and brief. It will go a whole lot better if the searching officer communicates with the person.

Do *not* assume the autistic person knows what is happening with their property; tell them it will be detained until they leave and tell them why: it is dangerous to keep the property, everybody has property taken off them, it is okay, they will get it back before they leave. Be extra patient with autistic people as they may have a 'lucky' or 'special' item they are never without and taking it away from them can be traumatic.

If upon searching anyone, an autism ID card is found, explore this further. Carers are usually the best source of information as they know the person better than anyone. Also feed the information back to the autistic person that their AA has been called. They may find some comfort in knowing that their carer is aware of their detention and will be attending.

This is not always the case as they may worry they are in greater trouble with the carer for being arrested. Reassurance on this matter is vital. Keep the lines of communication constantly open when dealing with anyone with autism. Remember: stress and anxiety lead to greater issues within custody.

Medication

A really important area to remember is an autistic person's possible need for medication. Whoever you bring into custody it is a priority that you ascertain what, if any, medication they require. I have seen so many officers present a detainee who they have brought from their H/A only to see the officer blanch when the DP has said they need their 'meds' whilst at the station.

Make it one of the first things you do, not just for autistic people but *all* detainees. Ask them when you have the opportunity what medication they are on and if they need it urgently *before* you enter the custody suite. If this means staying a bit longer at their H/A or taking a slight detour en route then do so. As I have already said, autistic people are statistically more likely to have co-morbid health conditions so there is a strong chance they will be on medication. Grabbing it now will not only save the custody staff more time (and possibly gain points with the sergeant), it will show the autistic person you are thinking about them and possibly open their channels of trust.

Do not under any circumstance allow the detainee to retain the medication. You have no idea what it is and even if it is legal. Once in custody report their existence to the sergeant and hand them over for a HCP to examine and assess if and when the DP requires them.

There have been many times when all investigation has halted because the person an officer has brought in needs to be taken immediately to hospital due to issues with medication. Do not allow this to happen to you.

Custody detention officers (CDOs)

The advent of CDOs several years ago came as a bitter blow to some of the police service; they saw it as another intrusion of their already shrinking world. Personally, I applauded it. The professionalism of my team was without reproach. Being a dedicated role, they learned to navigate the custody suite and its visitors, completely. As it was their only role, they saw issues that officers had missed; this was not out of neglect, but the CDOs were resident 24/7 and it was in their interest to notice these things. One of the most valuable aspects was the rapport they could quickly build with the detained person. The lack of a uniform with 'police' written on it helped to break down barriers which otherwise would have remained.

Their use cannot be underestimated. Many times they spotted life-threatening hazards way before they actually occurred. If they are trained in autism and the use of this book is extended to them, their ever-vigilant eyes could be crucial in identifying neurodiversity on your behalf.

If you are visiting a person with autism in a cell and they are told they will be spoken to in 5 minutes, make it 5 minutes. They may be counting the seconds until someone returns. Trust is fragile and can be broken all too easily. However, it can be gained quite quickly. Small, simple steps can calm them down sufficiently to make their detention bearable.

Having dealt with someone who is constantly on the intercom buzzer or banging on the hatch asking for the world, it is frustrating when you have done all that you can. People with autism often fall into this area; however most of the time it is due to anxiety. Relieve the anxiety and the stress can reduce. It is down to the short work done for the long term gain.

Confinement is a stressful and boring time for everyone in custody. For autistic people it can be crushing. The cell will be unfamiliar and distressing. The toilets are simply functional and can be off-putting causing them to withhold their bowel movements, which will make them uncomfortable and irritable. If this is spotted, reassure them the toilet is clean (even wipe it over with an antibacterial cloth in front of them) or wait until their carer arrives, have a chat with them and suggest that if they stood with the DP (a private chat is their legal right) in the cell, they may use the toilet. Just little thoughts like this will show the AA you are really looking after their loved one and may open up lines of communication previously closed.

If access to an exercise yard is available (taking into consideration weather and staffing) then allow them use of it, often if necessary. They may prefer it, they may not. Show them it. Tell them it exists; again do not assume they know. If it is their first time in custody then the chances are they won't. If they get in there and buzz to come out again by the time you reach the desk, do not lose patience; they may have spotted something you have not that has scared or unsettled them. Tell them it is okay and they can go back out again later if they want (if you have time).

This is not just pandering to a DP, causing unrest amongst your other regulars who will see/hear it and demand the same level of care. It is to prevent any escalation of their anxiety, which can lead to self-harm and suicide attempts (see later sections).

Removal of clothing for investigation purposes or because the DP has used them inappropriately will lead to extreme anxiety for an autistic person. The touch of a paper suit may feel like a cheese grater on their skin. It may genuinely not be possible for them to wear it. Keep calm, they are not being difficult. If a suicide attempt has not taken place, then furnish them with police issue replacements if possible or instruct their carer to bring in others from home; this will make them feel much better.

Similarly if it is appropriate to allow them a soft toy from home (or even their property) then consider it. If they are going to be in for some length of time, up to the first 24 hours or even longer, then revisit it. This is just a suggestion to add to the others contained within this book. It may seem ridiculous but it could just make your job that little bit easier.

Reading material can be a contentious point. Some custody sergeants loathe it and do not allow it as it impacts heavily on their time, others find it is a great calming aid. Either way, the choice lies with the sergeant. If the pile of dog-eared novels and crinkly newspapers is inappropriate for the person with autism, consider something from home again. The carer will probably be more than happy to bring something in. If this is not possible or you are waiting, have a look at the bottom of the unused pile of magazines in the store room, where the more 'uninteresting' ones lie. Here you find a more 'specialist' variety donated by someone with a particular interest, say 'steam train monthly' or 'knitting patterns weekly'.

Ask if the DP would like to look at these – you may find they would. Always use the term 'look at'. Reading may infer lots of words and boring stuff like that, which have a negative connotation. Mention that there are lots of pictures in them – it cannot do any harm. As with all cell additions, removal of the staples may be required.

Fingerprinting, DNA retrieval and photographing the person with autism

As part of the detention process you will have to obtain samples from the detainee, providing they have not been in custody before. The usual procedure is to photograph, take fingerprints and, if necessary, take a DNA sample.

This can be yet another flash point. STOP. THINK. ASSESS.

Put yourself in their situation. They have been arrested, transported and then booked into custody, asked numerous personal, possibly confusing questions, searched, had all of their property taken off them, put in horrible foam slippers and now you are demanding they sit still long enough for the next process.

It is an unpleasant situation for anyone to come into custody and have to endure this process but as you will now be aware it is even worse for autistic people who will be trying to cope with the increasing anxiety.

The procedure does *not* have to be done straight away; although it may be more convenient for you or the custody staff to do it right now, think about them. Could you wait until the AA arrives or let them sit down for a while in a quiet room or their cell?

Once again, ask *them*. Treat them with some sort of decency. If you can see they are suffering after the arrest then allow them a break before the next round of intrusive procedures happen.

If they are happy enough to do it then explain to them why the things have to be done and what happens to them. Tell them it is the law and has to be done. By communicating with them, you are engaging with them and showing them they are a valued human being.

Specific advice for custody sergeants

It is often said, 'A ship is steered from the helm'. The same can be said of a custody block.

Make it clear to your staff, and in particular any entering officers, that it is your block. You make the decisions and they *will* abide by them. If you say a DP is going to be treated in such a way then make sure that is reinforced. Too many times I have left an officer on constant watch or signed them out to an interview only to find they have upset the DP by doing the exact thing I forbade them to do. Tell the officer *clearly* what the rules are and that they are absolute.

If you speak clearly and politely to the person with autism, insist your staff do too. *Train* people around you; instruct them in how to deal with autism. You are the one spending your entire shift stuck in a concrete box, living with numerous 'customers'. If the officers and staff follow your lead, then you will know things will be done right. Remember, the officer will leave custody and you and your staff will be left to pick up the pieces after a bad incident.

This is not an insult, but advice: your knowledge of PACE is your saviour. Get to know it inside out. Know the sections pertinent to vulnerable people and juveniles. Be able to quote it back to legal representatives who may challenge you. Your confidence will reverberate through the rest of custody and provide a secure and safe environment.

By being fair, courteous and confident, you will gain the respect of people entering custody. Appropriate adults, solicitors, HCPs, social workers even PACE inspectors like to see a well-oiled machine being run efficiently by a good custody officer. Even if it is serene on the surface and you are spinning plates below, so be it. The outward calm must always prevail. From knowledge comes confidence and this leads to calmness. Knowing all you can about autism and using this book will help right across the board. The rules to deal with autism are exactly the same as dealing with any other minority. Treat them all with respect and as human beings and you will not go wrong.

Appropriate adults (AAs)

An AA is the person you will have a lot to do with whilst in custody or when taking a statement from an autistic person. They will be there to assist you, so use them and their knowledge to the best of your ability.

In the first instance an AA is usually a family member or carer close to the person with autism. However they can be from an institution they attend or another trusted friend. As long as the detainee is happy to have them present during questioning they do not have to have any formal qualifications to attend. It will be the custody officer's remit to explain the job of the AA upon their arrival. There are strict parameters which if they overstep can result in them being removed from the interview or other process the detainee is taking part in (for a full explanation of these please consult the Codes of Practice). Above all, their role is extremely important and it should be a positive one for the detainee.

PACE – appropriate adult

1.7 'The appropriate adult' means, in the case of a:

(b) a person who is vulnerable (see paragraph 1.4 and Note 1D):

i. *a relative, guardian or other person responsible for their care or custody;*

ii. *someone experienced in dealing with vulnerable persons but who is not:*

   ~ a police officer;

~ employed by the police;

~ under the direction or control of the chief officer of a police force;

~ a person who provides services under contractual arrangements (but without being employed by the chief officer of a police force), to assist that force in relation to the discharge of its chief officer's functions, whether or not they are on duty at the time.

iii. *failing these, some other responsible adult aged 18 or over who is other than a person described in the bullet points in sub-paragraph (b)(ii) above. See Note 1F. 1.7A The role of the appropriate adult is to safeguard the rights, entitlements and welfare of juveniles and vulnerable persons (see paragraphs 1.4 and 1.5) to whom the provisions of this and any other Code of Practice apply. For this reason, the appropriate adult is expected, amongst other things, to:*

- *support, advise and assist them when, in accordance with this Code or any other Code of Practice, they are given or asked to provide information or participate in any procedure;*

- *observe whether the police are acting properly and fairly to respect their rights and entitlements, and inform an officer of the rank of inspector or above if they consider that they are not;*

- *assist them to communicate with the police whilst respecting their right to say nothing unless they want to as set out in the terms of the caution (see paragraphs 10.5 and 10.6);*

   • *help them to understand their rights and ensure that those rights are protected and respected (see paragraphs 3.15, 3.17, 6.5A and 11.17).*

In addition to family, friends or care workers, many forces operate an 'in-house' scheme of volunteers who have been Disclosure and Barring Service (DBS) – formerly the Criminal Records Bureau (CRB) – checked and offer an out-of-hours service for persons detained who require interviewing.

Their role has been invaluable to me when all other avenues have failed; however their level of knowledge of autism must be explored before engaging them. Many of them may have received training or simply be willing to work with the detainee, others may not feel sufficiently qualified to assist. This is a valid concern and sourcing the appropriate AA with training in autism is always the best option.

Point out to the AA/carer that you only need *one* of them. They do tend to turn up in groups expecting to come in and wait. Explain politely that there is only room for one in custody; any more and the logistics become too vast to manage. Explain that you have many people in your custody and to keep everybody safe it is best to have only one at a time.

When a carer or family friend arrives to be an AA then make them welcome, no matter how difficult the DP has been; they are here to help *you*. Many times I have seen AAs standing in the corner and when asked they said they had been 'buzzed' in but then ignored. Don't do this. It could well be the first time they have been in a police station or indeed had any contact with the police. This is not a good first impression and may be counter-productive.

If at all possible take the AA to an interview room, give them a drink and sit them down. Make them feel welcome and comfortable before you launch into a monologue about the person with autism. They may have had a long drive, no sleep and they will definitely be feeling nervous. Explain slowly and clearly what has happened from start to finish, what you expect of them and what their rights in law are. Many custody officers simply assume knowledge on their part.

When the DP is brought to the desk to speak to the AA, they may react in a number of ways. They can be sullen, scared, excited or angry. These are all natural reactions. Direct the meeting firmly but do not chastise the DP (unless violent), but tell them in front of the AA that you expect them to behave in a calm and agreeable manner.

Confident use of ground rules is better for everyone involved and knowing where they stand can be reassuring for people with autism.

The AA is allowed to speak to the person with autism privately and *must* have this opportunity whilst in custody. For some reason, I have witnessed officers trying to discourage this, as if it is a clandestine operation. It is their right in law to do so. Open an interview room to them and allow the consultation to take place as you would with a legal representative.

If you can get to know the AA quickly, I advise doing so. Get them on your side and extract as much knowledge about the autistic person as possible. The more you know about the person you are going to deal with, the better. Their information about the person, and probably about autism in general, may be invaluable to your investigation.

Do not be afraid to ask the AA how the person you are about to deal with will react, what makes them comfortable and what makes them anxious. Use all of this information to form a package with which to assist the process, making it all flow more fluidly.

As set out in the Golden Rules, be polite, confident and flexible when dealing with the AA and autistic person. The AA may be more nervous than the detainee or person you are taking a statement from. Make them relaxed and tell them everything they need to know about the process you are conducting. Like the person with autism, treat them with the respect you would want for yourself.

Registered Intermediaries

Registered Intermediaries (RIs) may not be a name you are familiar with. You might not have ever heard of them or if you have, never had a chance to work with them. I will give their official explanations and allow you to explore their duties in more detail on the websites detailed below:

They are defined by the Department of Justice[1] as:

A Registered Intermediary is a self-employed communication specialist who helps vulnerable witnesses and complainants to give evidence to the police and to the court in criminal trials.

A witness might need the help of a Registered Intermediary because of their age, or a learning, mental or physical disability or disorder. They can often be the difference between a witness being able to give evidence or not.

The Crown Prosecution Service (CPS)[2] state:

The potential need for a RI should be identified as early as possible. This should, ideally, be done by the police officer during the course of the investigation with the RI being engaged prior to the witness being interviewed. However, it is still possible to engage a RI later in the process if it is considered that the quality of evidence from a witness can be improved at court. If communication issue/s are identified or raised post-charge, the CPS is responsible for ensuring that a RI is engaged.

---

1 At www.gov.uk
2 At www.cps.gov.uk

In light of the scarcity of RIs, the appropriateness of assessment must be decided with care to ensure their availability for those witnesses and defendants who are most in need. Once the possible need for a RI has been identified, the Witness Intermediary Service (WIS) should be contacted. The WIS is operated on behalf of the Ministry of Justice (MoJ) by the National Crime Agency (NCA) through its Specialist Operations Centre.

This new service has been made available for vulnerable adults who are witnesses, and, at the discretion of the trial judge, can be extended to the defendant.

What I would like to see is more RIs to aid the communication between the police and autistic people. Their expertise would be invaluable to an investigation for a victim, witness or even an alleged offender. With more investment the whole CJS could be assisted by their expansion to more areas.

Interviewing autistic people

The interview of an autistic person is in itself fairly straightforward. The rules that govern your usual interview will basically apply to theirs. Where the difference lies is in overlaying some fundamental principles which will assist both them and you in achieving a successful conclusion.

I will not insult you by suggesting an interview plan or even a crib sheet and move on to taking care of the autistic person during the process, which is where I have found the biggest knowledge gap with officers.

There are many different styles of interviewing, some of which you will prefer to others. No matter which you choose remember who you have in front of you and consider every part of the interview in stages, giving the next as much thought as the previous one.

The first part of this interviewing section is the law. Unfortunately I still have to outline the legislation so we all know where we stand. It is just as well you know these important rules and can quote them back if necessary.

PACE – Codes of practice state:

> *11.15 A juvenile or vulnerable person must not be interviewed regarding their involvement or suspected involvement in a criminal offence or offences, or asked to provide or sign a written statement under caution or record of interview, in the absence of the appropriate adult unless paragraphs 11.1 or 11.18 to 11.20 apply. See Note 11C.*
>
> *11C Although juveniles or vulnerable persons are often capable of providing reliable evidence, they may, without knowing or wishing to do so, be particularly prone in certain circumstances to providing information that may be unreliable, misleading or self-incriminating. Special care should always be taken when questioning such a person, and the appropriate adult should be involved if there is any doubt about a person's age, mental state or capacity. Because of the risk of unreliable evidence it is also important to obtain corroboration of any facts admitted whenever possible. Because of the risks, which the presence of the appropriate adult is intended to minimise, officers of superintendent rank or above should exercise their discretion under paragraph 11.18(a) to authorise the commencement of an interview in the appropriate adult's absence only in exceptional cases, if it is necessary to avert one or more of the specified risks in paragraph 11.1.*

There are times where an officer not below the rank of superintendent *can* authorise an interview without an AA, if the circumstances are so extreme that the delay of the interview would jeopardise the investigation to such an extent that serious harm, loss of property or the escape of an offender would occur.

Personally I only ever saw one of these; they are extremely rare but can occur. More usually the interview is delayed and the AA is present.

Building on the above, all interviews and in fact any dealings with vulnerable people must be conducted with great care and compassion. The person being dealt with, either in or outside of custody, will be feeling stressed. This anxiety, as you are now aware, will build the longer they are within the bounds of an unfamiliar establishment. However, the presence of their AA could be sufficient to calm them enough to talk to you or the interview team.

Here are a few suggestions for investigating/interviewing officers to consider:

- Prior preparation of the interview room should be always considered. Look at the lighting, temperature (autistic people can be very sensitive to a room too bright or dark, too hot or too cold), the layout of the room (could the door suddenly be opened, hitting the person?).

- Do not plan lengthy interviews if at all possible. The stress of the interview will be draining for them; making it longer could be detrimental and answers less forthcoming. Have several breaks with drinks or even meals arranged for their comfort.

- Explain what is going to happen in the interview. Do not overlook even a small detail as it may be the one thing the person is fixating on. If it is a disc recording system, tell them that or if they are on CCTV let them know; it might be a positive for them.

- Tell them you will be asking them some questions and when you are finished you will tell them the interview is going to end. Ask them if they have any questions for you.

- Say the caution slowly, explaining it and ensuring the person realises it is legally binding.

- Remind them of their legal rights and entitlements.

- Keep all questions simple. Do not try to 'trip' the person up with complex, wordy or confusing questions.

- Do not use slang, sarcasm, idioms (e.g. 'were you over the moon?'), acronyms or 'police speak'.

- Do not use open questions, such as 'Tell me what you did this morning.' You are likely to get an inventory from the moment they awoke, including putting on their slippers.

- Use closed questions designed to elicit a specific response: 'What happened when you tried to pay for the chocolate in the shop?' This may get the reply you require, for example, 'The man was nasty to me.'

- Tell them when they give you something you want, 'that was a really good description of the park, thank you. What did the man look like?' It is not praising an offender; it is prompting a positive line of thought. Autistic people sometimes do not receive any positive response in their day-to-day lives.

- Have questions written out in advance to shorten the pauses in the interview. Silence can be deafening for a person with autism or they can lose attention quickly if not stimulated.

- At the same time, do not ask too many questions or fire them out too fast; give the person time to answer. Work sensitively around speech impediments, which can be embarrassing.

- If it is possible, interview them with only one officer; more people in the room may raise the stress level unnecessarily.

- If they require something to calm them (an item in their property) and it is safe to do so, allow them to hold it. Anything they feel is familiar could allow them to cope with this already incredibly stressful situation. However a conversation with the AA prior may be prudent about how they may react to having to return it back into their property.

- Plan for more time than you usually would. This cushion will allow any unforeseen incidents to be encompassed. Autistic people may need extra time to adjust, process and absorb the information they are being bombarded with. Allow them this time. If you are stressed by time, they will be.

- Once the interview has been terminated, tell the person this. Explain that the questioning is over and you will not be asking them any more today. Anxiety will rise if they think they may be questioned again.

- Ask the AA if they wish to talk to the person with autism alone, again. They may not know they can. Also if there is going to be time, refresh their drinks or offer food, as now the interview is over and the pressure has reduced they might be relaxed enough to eat. The same applies to comfort breaks, like toileting or an exercise yard visit.

You may have finished the interview and now be ready for the next stage but the person with autism will not. If you are going to sort out bail with the sergeant, tell them and ask them if they would like some down time whilst you organise it.

When you have completed the charges or the bail explain it clearly first to the AA, so they can simplify it if necessary. They will not be able to do this if they haven't got a clue what 47(3) bail is. Remember: do not cut corners or use jargon, and speak clearly and carefully. There can be a need for the autistic person to process what has just happened at every stage and this may take a little time. Do not take this as pandering to the DP but simply aiding the communication between everyone in custody, which is what you should be aiming for in each of your visits.

Presumed innocence

Throughout the investigation, be mindful of a full and frank confession. Autistic people often like to please those they feel are in power. Probe further and check they have all of the facts correct. A straight forward 'yes' may seem like a detection in the bag, but you could be charging the wrong person.

If the admission is true, look at the reasons behind it. Have they committed the offence due to bullying, bribery, suggestion or as a stooge? Autistic people can be extremely vulnerable and commit crime sometimes as they see no other solution or genuinely do not realise it is an offence at all.

Another stereotype is that people with autism do not commit crime or they are all innocent. This is completely untrue. As with any other section of society, there are those who are and those who are not. Some people with autism deliberately commit crime, plan it and have no regrets, just as neurotypical offenders do. Having been dealt with on several occasions, they may have perfected a strategy which plays on NT emotions and this presumed innocence. Probing behind their façade will require investigation but may prove worthwhile.

As with all persons in custody, check out the facts and present them in exactly the same way as you usually would. Treating an autistic person in the way I prescribe does not prevent a thorough investigation, it just 'bolts on top' to ensure their fair treatment whenever in custody.

The right disposal?

When the interviews are concluded and all of the available evidence is placed before you, the choice of how to deal with the person with autism arises. The statements may have been difficult to obtain or the interview may have been a nightmare but how the DP is disposed of must be the right disposal, for everyone.

Placing an autistic person before the courts may be exactly the right choice; however, searching behind the crime and delving into exactly why they committed it might steer the disposal in another direction. To this end, it could be the right disposal.

You are taught not to assume anything: check and check again. Deal with the facts alone. Sometimes taking another look at these facts can build a picture that when you stand back reveals something underlying and previously missed.

In the next example, I wanted to show you that by working with a person with autism and their family, the correct result for an investigation could be more straightforward than you expect.

EXAMPLE 8

Daniel is a 14-year-old boy with Asperger's who attends mainstream school. He keeps himself to himself and has no real friends; however, this suits Daniel. Since joining the school in the last academic year his work has seen a steady improvement and his integration into school life has been good. Up until now he has been an exemplary pupil.

Teachers begin to notice bouts of anger from Daniel, particularly after break times and lunch. When back in class his attention is brief and interspersed by aggression. No one can find out why. Daniel will not talk about it. This continues for a couple of weeks with his behaviour quickly declining.

One Saturday afternoon Daniel is unexpectedly invited to another child's house. His parents are delighted. Daniel shows little interest, but attends as requested. Upon his return Daniel explains it was a pleasant experience as Mike had a new gaming console which he found enjoyable and his bedroom was full of items Daniel would like. Mike's parents said he had been a delight to have and would welcome him back, anytime.

The next day Daniel goes out to play locally and is back by the time set by his parents. Nothing seems unusual and he washes and prepares for dinner without incident.

After school on Monday evening Daniel's parents are visited by a police officer:

'I need to talk to Daniel. Is he in?'

'Why?' Daniel's dad demands.

'I have received information that your son may be responsible for a burglary yesterday and I need to take him to the station for an interview,' the officer replies.

'There must have been a mistake, Daniel isn't a criminal,' his mother responds.

The officer explains a complaint has been made and that the best place for it to be investigated is the police station. Daniel is booked in voluntarily and the interview (without a solicitor as the parents presume Daniel is innocent) begins:

'Do you know Mike?'

'Yes,' he replies, 'I went to play with him on Saturday.'

'Do you know Mike's house has been broken into?'

'Yes.'

'How?'

The officer receives no reply. 'Did you go back there yesterday?' they ask.

'Yes.'

'Why?' asks the officer.

'To get the things I had seen in his bedroom.' Daniel's parents look at him in horror.

'Why?' continues the officer. Daniel does not reply. The officer repeats the question. Daniel refuses to reply. 'Why won't you say?' asks the officer. Daniel stares ahead, refusing to reply. His dad interrupts and asks Daniel to answer. Daniel refuses to speak.

'Where is the property now?' asks the officer.

'Safe,' Daniel replies.

'What do you mean by safe?' asks the officer.

'It is safe,' he replies again.

'Why did you choose Mike's house?' asks the officer following another direction.

'I knew exactly where his things were,' he replies.

'Why didn't you take anything else?'

'Because it wasn't what I needed,' Daniel replies.

'What did you need?' the officer asks.

'Mike's things.'

'Why?' the officer tries again. Daniel refuses to answer.

'How did you know Mike's house would be empty?' asks the officer.

'They said they were going swimming and maybe I might like to go next time.'

'Yet you smashed the window and stole Mike's stuff even after they were nice to you? Why?' the officer asked. Daniel does not reply.

'What did you smash the window with?' the officer asks.

'A brick I found near the rabbit hutches. I saw a man do it on TV.'

'What did you take from Mike's room?'

'His games console, the games for it, his watch, his iPad, his iPod,' Daniel replies without effort.

'Why just them? There was lots of other stuff to take in the house, really valuable stuff.'

'Mike's things are what I needed.'

Perplexed, the officer concludes the interview and explains to the parents that without the return of the property and with a full admission, the case, even though a first offence, may have to go to court. Horrified, they plead for time to speak to their son. They return to the interview room and speak privately with Daniel. After ten minutes they emerge and report that he still refuses to give any further information. Daniel is released but told he may be interviewed again.

At school the next day Mike charges up to Daniel. 'What the hell did you take my stuff for? I thought we were friends? You broke my dad's window and really upset my mum.'

Daniel listens intently, then replies, 'Your stuff is safe.'

This confuses Mike who asks, 'What does that mean, safe? Where is it? What have you done with it?' Daniel refuses to explain any further and the bell goes to signal end of break.

Mike can't get Daniel's strange reply out of his head so informs the teachers and then his parents when he gets home. Mike's parents are good people so they inform the police officer that they are concerned all is not as it seems and they would like the officer to investigate further. They also go on to say that the rabbits they keep had been let out of their hutches on the same day, which is strange.

These new facts are fed back to Daniel's parents, who are just as confused but worried that their previously angelic child has gone off the rails so badly. They ask him again to tell them what he has done with Mike's stuff, but he adamantly refuses to reply.

After a week, it looks more likely that Daniel will end up in court with a criminal record and exclusion from school.

Meanwhile, Mike has been watching Daniel, in and out of school, as he feels there is something not right going on. Travelling home on the bus one evening, he sees three lads from his year surround Daniel and start to threaten him: 'Listen doom brain, if you don't get the money or something valuable by Friday we will kick your teeth in, got that?' To reinforce the threat, they each punch him. Daniel takes the abuse and simply looks out of the window. He gets off at the next stop, so does Mike. Mike follows Daniel to a small wooded area by his home but unfortunately loses him inside.

Mike returns home quickly to tell his parents what he has learned. A meeting is arranged between both families at Daniel's home, where after reassuring him they are there to help, the truth is finally revealed.

Daniel explains that the three lads are bullying him. They had started off with just pushes and trips but it has progressed to threats of violence if they aren't paid in cash or goods to leave him alone. After his savings ran out, he found he had no option but to seek funding from another source, knowing his parents would see immediately if something in his house went missing. The bullies at school had told him to break into a house, which is exactly what he did.

When asked why he chose Mike's he explains that it was the most logical; no one was going to be in and he knew exactly where the property he could take was situated.

Daniel then takes both families to the woods near their house, explaining it was the safest place to hide the goods from the bullies until he had thought of a plan to dispose of them. He pushes some bushes and leaves aside to show a natural hollow under a fallen tree trunk.

There, underneath it, is a perfectly tied black bin liner. Daniel explains the plastic was protecting the property from moisture, the goods were in a box to save them from harm and they had each been wrapped in clothing to keep them safe.

He had not worked out how to sell them; he had not wished to give them directly to the bullies because that was wrong as they did not belong to him, but turning them into money to give them was acceptable. The police are called, the complaint withdrawn and the damaged window paid for by Daniel's parents.

Criminalising Daniel now makes no sense. He had a legal argument of extreme provocation. In his mind, he did the act to stop another from applying violence to him. On top of that he is autistic and has a very logical mind. He was being bullied, he needed a solution and this was the most logical one, which was suggested by the aggressors. It could even be argued that he did not have the requisite Mens rea to commit the offence in the first place.

The right disposal would be No Further Action. You have no complaint and the property has been returned. I know this would not happen. No force is going to give up a detection without a fight.

So, the only other option would be a warning. An offence has still taken place and it could not be struck out as No Crime on the system, so an 'out-of-custody' disposal is the only decision. Daniel receives the lowest punishment possible. Although his actions can be rationalised, it does not excuse a criminal result.

Daniel should be told that he does not need to keep bullying to himself, but to report it and the officer should now be working with the school to prevent this happening again. Daniel's parents may also wish to seek further support from voluntary organisations in their area and these should be offered to them by the officer.

Purely for continuity's sake in the example, imagine the bullies were excluded, the families remained in close contact from then on and Daniel never again put a foot wrong...and perhaps when asked about the rabbits, he said he didn't like to see animals in cages so set them all free.

Charging/formal cautioning an autistic person

Exactly the same rules apply for charging someone as booking them in or interviewing them. Be clear what is occurring, speak slowly and clearly, repeat anything if asked. Be one hundred per cent certain they understand the caution and its legal implications before charging.

Explain what the charge(s) are line by line; leave nothing ambiguous. Once at home they may worry constantly about the charges, especially if they have misconstrued what you have said.

Make sure they know they are now required to attend court, when it is and at what time. Their AA/legal representative will be fully aware but so must the person you are charging.

When handing over the paper charges, highlight the court details and time to make doubly sure. Once complete ask them if there is anything else you can do. Escort them to at least the door if not their car and see them off the premises if you can. This courtesy will make the AA feel slightly better if not the person charged; after all, the AA has done nothing wrong.

If administering a formal caution or fixed penalty notice be sure to explain all of the above and in addition, tell them it now means they have a police record. Many officers fail to clarify this. Cautions may be disclosed to current or prospective employers and must be declared if the person is involved in certain roles such as working with children or vulnerable adults. Cautions are also made available to the Disclosure and Barring Service. Accepting a caution can affect someone's ability to travel and work outside the European Union, with some countries reserving the right to refuse entry visas. It is a serious disposal and they might prefer to take their chance in court.

Bail

If you are going to impose conditions on autistic people, please make them crystal clear and appropriate. On far too many occasions I have been asked by an officer to consider bail conditions (before or after charge) that are wholly inappropriate for the detainee (and in particular an autistic person) to adhere to.

This is a real example:

Not to contact or communicate in any way with Dave Bloggs.

Not to be within 50 metres of Dave Bloggs or their home address.

Dave Bloggs is the injured party but lives next door! This is a complete waste of time. The autistic person has absolutely no chance of complying with these conditions. As soon as they go home, they have breached them and will be arrested. Do not set them up to fail. If bail conditions are really necessary then choose ones they can stick to.

Also explain *how* they can stick to them. Give them advice of alternative routes or places they can go without breaching their bail. The autistic person may not have any other routes in their head. That route that takes them right past the injured party's (IP's) house might be the only one they have ever used. Consider using routes in the conditions which they have to adhere to or show them on a map (and give them a copy!) those that are appropriate and acceptable.

Explain patiently they have these conditions to protect *them* as well as the IP. I have seen many officers miss this little gem. By explaining that the conditions give clear instructions to both parties and it is for their benefit too, it can sometimes be accepted more readily.

As with the charges, ensure that all parties have a copy of the bail conditions and are clear what happens next. Take your time with them and explain everything, several times if necessary.

Self-harm and suicide

If you have charged an autistic person and refused bail, the likelihood of self-harm or suicide is going to be higher due to their increased levels of anxiety. This section concerning custody is a serious matter and always distressing for all involved. This area of autism, and indeed in any part of life in general, is an extremely sensitive subject matter. The reasons for someone deliberately harming their own body are intensely private and varied: control, release and emotional pain are but a few. In this next section, I will attempt to highlight some of the thought processes behind it.

Self-harm can manifest early in life; children do it and can continue until old age. There is nothing to say it is something that happens for a set period of time or until intervention occurs. The act of harming can be a quick process over in seconds or can last hours. It completely depends on the person and circumstances behind it.

Thoughts which lead to self-harm can spring from many situations or the environment around the person. In people with autism this can be amplified due to an inability or wish not to communicate with the people and world around them. The frustration that friends, carers, social workers or anyone they meet fail to understand or recognise their feelings can cause a pain, mentally or physically, which eventually festers away, forming a darkness where the only release is self-harm.

There may be no clear explanation for it and the autistic person may not be able to effectively verbalise it. Someone without autism will find it hard to cement the complex feelings and emotions involved in their self-harm, so someone with autism who fears ridicule or rejection may find it impossible to divulge to a stranger why they do it.

Taking themselves away to a private space, controlling how they self-harm and having complete control over the act can be an overwhelming urge; something that they have started as a simple release may become an addiction. The act may no longer be the focus of the self-harm, it may become the only thing they have any say or control over. The sudden rush of endorphins being sent to the pain receptors could be the only real feeling they can comprehend but the exact reasons behind the self-harm may never be uncovered.

Self-harm can also take another subtler route. It can happen without consciously knowing it. For instance take the mouth. This area is usually closed off from public view, safe, private. In times of extreme stress, many people chew at the soft inner cheek area without even knowing it, not perceiving they are in fact self-harming. It may never be recognised as these times are rare in a peaceful world. The more stress caused or anxiety felt, the more the chewing may occur. People with autism can feel a lot of stress and anxiety.

When biting at the flesh inside the mouth, cheeks, lips or tongue, it can cause an immense pain. It can also be controlled by the teeth, by the person. What they do in there is away from prying eyes and no one need know about it. If the person with autism is in an extreme situation it could be this that they turn to before anything else, as it is immediate feedback.

It is here that you as an officer may suddenly see blood trickling (or in some cases rushing) from the mouth. It may not be from an external source.

DO NOT PANIC. STOP. THINK.

Is the autistic person doing this deliberately?

If possible, ask them if they are okay. Talk to them. Reassure them. *Do not* become angry with them or assume anything. This is a very stressed person; the fact that an officer is in front of them may be the only reason they are stressed enough to self-harm. It could be their own perception of guilt. Two weeks ago, they may have taken an extra biscuit from the table in the day centre, and assume you are there to 'lock them up' for it. Of course, you are not, so tell them why you are there; *talk* to them.

After self-harming the person may feel a short-term sense of release due to the stinging, tingling or pins and needles; however it may feel to them this will be transitory. The cause of their distress is still likely to be there and needs to be confronted at some time or another. Self-harm can also stir up even more dark, difficult emotions, which can cause the circle of pain to spin on, possibly making them feel worse.

Whatever the reasons are behind the self-harm, it is important to know that with self-harm come risks. Once started there is a real chance of dependence on self-harm, and even with help it can take a long time to stop. Any person dealt with who is self-harming should always be directed to appropriate support agencies that can assist them.

Self-harm in custody

Having seen an awful lot of self-harm whilst in the confines of custody, it soon became apparent that it may not have been just the incarceration that was causing my 'customers' to do it. I spoke at length to a few of the people who did it, whether watched constantly or not. Most I have to say were neurodiverse or had diagnosed mental health issues.

After a considerable amount of work, I was able to speak to them honestly about what they did and why they did it. I was surprised that the answers were often very clear. Most apologised for causing me extra work and appreciated the stress it caused my staff and me. They went on to articulate that they had no control over it and did it whenever they felt the need; if this be in custody (particularly in custody when treated badly) then so be it.

There have been extreme examples (far too graphic for publication) of how the person self-harming got the item, usually razor blades, into custody, evading the metal detectors I had installed to try and prevent any concealment.

This shows how serious a person who self-harms takes it and their ability to have items readily to hand with which to carry it out. Their actions and thoughts should never be dismissed as purely attention-seeking or bluffs. Having been caught out once on this, I vowed never again.

By following the advice in this book, particularly the main custody section, the times self-harm occurs can be reduced. I advocated explaining to anyone with Police National Computer (PNC) 'markers' that I was aware of the fact and was available to talk to at any point to prevent them needing to do it whilst in my custody. A lot acknowledged they had problems and the openness of my address gave them confidence to state that they were okay or not at that time and to request that an HCP be called. Some stated they were okay when it was clear that they were not. A person with autism may not be able to verbalise their feelings during the booking-in process; however, a visit to their cell shortly after may have given them time to process the questions and hopefully talk about their issues.

A clear sign of self-harm are the marks that are left behind. These, once recognised, are unmistakable and must be treated with caution. I have seen some people who enter custody with ladders of scars all over their arms, legs and even the rest of their body. Some will openly state they are old and there are no current problems, others will deny their origins. Either is a red flag and something to note on the record and investigate. Call an HCP; this is always the safest option.

Having officers on constant watch, with door open or on camera, is a massive drain on resources. It is also toxic for the person detained if immediately upon their arrival they have someone sitting at their cell door (usually the arresting or transporting officer) looking at everything they do. This action alone can push them into a 'corner' where the only option they have is to fight back by aggression or withdrawal (under a blanket is the usual technique). Neither is a helpful result.

Explain to the autistic person why you are placing them on constant watch, tell them that it is for their safety and you will be calling an HCP to check on their welfare. Be open with them and deal with their concerns. Hiding a visit from an HCP can cause them instant anxiety when they arrive. If they are going to escalate their behaviour then it is going to happen anyway, but giving them time to process the fact can be the lifeline they might need.

Sometimes there is nothing anyone can do to help the DP. They have a mindset where they are going to be as destructive as possible, either to themselves or the environment around them. Even when this happens and tensions rise, there is still a way back to navigate the issues. Re-engaging with them, even though this seems an undesirable thing to do, could open channels of communication once again.

A person with autism can find it extremely difficult to break a mindset. It may be their default position and they are unable or unwilling to drop the imaginary wall around them, letting someone, especially anyone they don't know, in to their 'safe' area. It is this skill that carers have developed over years of practice and even then, it does not always work. A major tool used to aid re-engagement is patience. This is easier said than done in a busy custody block with all of the constraints placed upon its staff. Even if the sergeant or detention officers have to leave it until they physically have the time to try again with the autistic person, just revisiting them with a fresh perspective could be the lifeline they need.

Staying calm pays dividends. You don't need to smile or be jolly; this is sometimes counterproductive. Pulling the hatch down, asking if they are okay, if they need a drink, if you can come in and have a word are all things that work. Asking for permission to enter one of your own cells, in your custody block, seems ridiculous. However, you will be amazed how many times it works.

Imagine you are the one sitting in the cell and have been 'ragged' around by people you didn't want to meet, never mind touch. You have been booked into a huge, noisy building and pushed into a smelly room you cannot leave. How would you feel? Aggrieved, pissed off, resentful? And why wouldn't you? Then the huge metal door bangs open and this big person in uniform starts shouting questions at you (it can be very noisy in custody, so shouting is the norm). Wouldn't you be scared? I would.

Look at the difference with my scenario:

Slide the hatch down gently – dropping it down with a bang is a shock (and it damages the runners).

Introduce yourself; they may have forgotten who you are.

Are you okay? Want a drink? If yes, then tell them you will get them one or if you are really lucky someone else may make it whilst you deal with the DP.

Do you mind that I come in? Is that okay? If yes, acknowledge it...'great'. If no then ask why; this may be what you have been suspecting. If all you receive is a stream of abuse, leave but go back again later, then try it again; eventually it may work. The thing with custody is you have 24 hours to win the war of attrition.

Assuming you have received a positive reply (or at least not sputum or abuse) then open the door carefully, again assuming they are not just behind the door waiting to pounce.

Before walking in, speak to them again and make sure it is slower and softer than usual. Use all of the Golden Rules, even in the cell.

Ask them to sit if they are standing to make them more at ease. If you feel comfortable doing it, hunker down, keeping your back towards the door and away from the DP. Being on the same level reduces intimidation.

Ask how they are, how they are coping and if there is anything they need. I am not trying to teach granny how to suck eggs here; these are just reminders or prompts. What I will reiterate is to watch for their responses. Non-verbal cues. Autistic people can appear to avoid eye contact; this is not a sign of guilt, it can be genuinely painful to look at people. Any avoidance to answer a question may not be purposeful, it could be confusion. After waiting a short while you may want to rephrase the question and see what that brings.

Above all, stay *calm*. *Listen* to what they say. Tell them you *believe* them. Tell them what is happening and *do not lie* to them. This will destroy all of the good work you may have done.

One thing that used to frustrate me was when an officer deliberately lied to someone they were presenting; 'It will be a five-minute job, mate' was the worst, 'In and out, mate' was another, knowing that they had statements to take or investigation to do. I was then left with a detainee who was furious because I was refusing them bail on the officer's request.

Autistic people will take what you say literally. If you know it is going to take hours to investigate the offence, then tell them that; 'You will be here for quite a while' is vague enough to placate them for the time being. Don't tell them it'll only be half an hour or so when you know that they are in for the night.

Trust is a huge thing and can be the gossamer thread onto which the person with autism is clinging. Break the trust, you break the thread. This could lead straight to self-harm or even worse.

Watch for signs that your detainee is declining. If the person with autism has been refused bail or is being placed before the courts, then the chance of self-harm or worse escalates. Ask the CDOs to look closer on your behalf and take extra care at every point where their detention is extended. It may be that they were willing to stave off self-harm until they were away from custody but now may not be able to control it any longer.

Treat the person with autism with care and respect, stick to the Golden Rules and follow the advice in this book and you might stop this destructive behaviour. If at any point you feel unhappy with their demeanour call in an HCP and ask for their advice.

Suicide

The last section in this area is something that impacts on custody daily and I feel needs to be discussed. Suicide attempts are a serious, stressful and dangerous event that all custody staff dread. No matter how much training you have had, the first time you see a DP with something tied around their neck will stay with you the rest of your life (it has me). That initial icy feeling as a thought runs through your head, 'Are they dead?' is heart-stopping.

You could have done everything in this book and been a new best buddy to the DP – it will not stop someone from trying to take their own life. Being charged with a serious offence or refusal of bail has been all it has taken to prompt the attempt. Even an unsuccessful phone call can be the catalyst.

However, there are things that can be done for people with autism. Access to their carer or AA is an excellent choice. They are the people who can advise you on how best to judge their moods. You may completely miss a downward spiral. Speak to them yourself if the possibility of a personal visit is not viable.

If the person has tried it before then take the information seriously. Do not overlook the chance of it happening again. If the person with autism did it last time they were in, there is a good chance they may do it again. The situation is exactly the same in their mind, only the day has changed.

Watch them closely, even raise their observation level for an hour or so; the extra visits may just be enough to reassure them.

At any change in the judicial process watch their responses and even their AA: the emotions of one may feed the other. I have witnessed an AA react badly to a charge which in turn upset the DP. The AA/carer is not perfect and under a lot of stress. Giving them the heads up before the event can alleviate any unnecessary problem. Keep everyone in the loop.

As I have mentioned previously, hiding under their blanket is extremely frustrating, and worrying when they have self-harm or suicide markers. There is little to be done apart from removing it. If you feel strongly enough, then remove it. Be aware that the person with autism may only be hiding from the strong lights in the cell. If it is possible to lower them (night lights, etc.), then ask the person if they will have their head remain above the blanket if the lights are turned down. Think about what you can do to relieve their stress but maintain safety for you.

Be open and honest with the autistic person. Trying to deceive them is not a good option and it may even result in the situation becoming irretrievable. Tell them what is happening, be flexible and voice your concerns about their behaviour if it helps.

Follow the Golden Rules. Be fair and respectful with the autistic person and hopefully you will never have to see anything that will stay with you forever.

The police fan

This last section can be technically squeezed into custody because of the repeated arrests that occur with police fans, and it also rounds off the section with something you may not have thought about.

What if you have to deal with an autistic person who adores the police and everything about them? They could be a witness or an offender. There have been several cases where the offender deliberately re-offends with usually petty or low-level crime to become embroiled with the law. This also spills over into other areas you deal with but l will concentrate with those surrounding autism.

The obsession can stem from any number of beginnings; the darkest can be abuse, where the victim seeks help from the police or can see them as a route out of the desperate situation. It can be simply a fascination with all of the shiny toys the police carry.

The obsession may just as well be about any of the emergency services or indeed hospitals. I am concentrating on the police aspect as it is they who will ultimately be the ones dealing with this person.

Having a suspect sitting in the rear of your car with a huge grin on their face can be an unsettling experience, particularly if they have handcuffs on which seem to be pleasing them a little bit more. I will step aside from the sexual element to any restraint, as the person who derives any gratification from the arrest process – although it is possible they are autistic – is likely to have other mental health issues that I am not qualified to discuss. I have encountered such individuals during an investigation but the details are not applicable to this book. When first meeting the person with autism, all of the Golden Rules are relevant and you should proceed exactly as I have advised. Sometimes with an autistic person it may quickly become apparent that they are engaging, possibly fully. This may be a good thing but in itself should be a trigger for your thought patterns:

Is the person engaging? Yes.

Do they understand why I am here? Yes.

Do they seem happy and relaxed? Yes.

This is going well. You don't need the Golden Rules. STOP. THINK.

Why are they fully engaging? Why are they happy? Seek answers if possible from their carer or someone who knows them well. Are they usually like this? If so, then great, you have hit the jackpot and the arrest/interview is going to be a doddle. If not, then prepare for a more involved investigation.

In the next example I am going to show you what an initial petty offence could be covering when involved with a repeat offender, but one who is more than happy to accompany you to the station.

EXAMPLE 9

The offence you are investigating is a minor criminal damage. Two fence panels were kicked through by a young lad, who stayed just long enough before running off that the injured party (IP) could tell who it was. They know the lad; he is called Jason. He lives just around the corner with the rest of his family. He has never been a problem to the IP before, although they have heard he can be a 'bit of a one' from local gossip.

You do some background checks on the address, which reveal lots of calls of a similar nature, but also mention in one serial the word autism. You arrive at the house and see a young man fitting the description standing in the window, waving at you with a big smile on his face. The first thought in your head could be, 'The cheeky swine.' Others may simply dismiss the action as bravado. At this point, the Golden Rules should be already kicking in. STOP. THINK.

In the first instance the IP has given you a valuable piece of information: Jason can be 'a bit of a one'. What does that mean? It could mean that he is just a usual lad, a bit of a tearaway, high spirited or it could mean he may be neurodiverse. Just keep an open mind.

You are greeted by Jason's mum, standing on the door step, arms folded. She gives you another good indication about his previous behaviour: 'Oh, it's you lot again. What's he supposed to have done now?'

This tells you that it isn't the first time she has had to deal with the police and she is already defensive. This is a completely ordinary reaction that you will probably have met countless times before. The first thing going through your head is possibly, 'Here we go, another mother who is anti-police and a vile kid.'

STOP. THINK.

This woman may have had to deal with Jason's obsessive behaviour for the last 18 years. You have no idea what she lives with on a daily basis; the prejudice and the attitude of the officers attending regularly are draining for her. Jason is a big lad and she can only do so much to control him. THINK. What are social services, local health and your force doing to help?

Your first words are going to dictate how this will go. You can either go with:

'I am here to deal with a report of criminal damage to some fence panels. Your lad Jason has been named as the offender. I am going to need an interview down the nick with him.'

The response you get is, 'He is always blamed for everything around here cos they all know him. It ain't him, he's been in all morning.'

The shutters have gone up and she is already defending her son. This response has been tuned from years of dealing with many false claims against Jason but also his obsession. Perhaps you could try another angle:

'Morning, you alright? I have a bit of a job I need to talk to you and Jason about. Any chance of coming inside? You don't want the neighbours listening, do you?'

The response this time is, 'Oh. Alright then chuck, come on in, don't mind the house, it's a bloody tip. I ain't got time to turn round these days.'

Instantly her demeanour has changed. Why? You have used her in the equation. Nobody does this; they focus on Jason and the problem they have come to resolve. By stepping back and actually considering her, you have gone a long way in trying to deal with the bigger issues. By inviting you in, she is saying that she is trusting you. Build on this and do not make rash decisions to reverse it.

Jason's mum, Denise, shows you through to the front room. Jason is there and smiles at you again, giving you a little wave. Denise speaks to him, 'What have you been up to now, Jason? This nice man has come to talk to us and they don't come for nothing, do they?'

Jason shakes his head. You assume this is in response to her question not his position on guilt. Seizing the opportunity, you engage directly with Jason: 'Hi, Jason, I am PC Bloggs. I have come to talk to you and your mum about something that happened today. Is that okay?'

By taking this route, you have acknowledged Jason and shown his mum you are a person of your word. Jason naturally wants to talk to you, that's why you are here. In his mind, it is exactly what he wants. Jason nods and smiles more broadly.

You explain to mum, in Jason's presence, about the panels, that he will have to be interviewed about this at the station and you will need her help.

She rolls her eyes and sighs. She has been through this far too many times. Nodding she looks sadly at Jason, then at you, 'Can I show something, officer?'

'Of course you can, Denise.'

She escorts you upstairs to Jason's bedroom. The walls are covered in police posters and there is paraphernalia all around the room. She explains Jason is autistic and how it affects him. Now, you begin to see, there could be more to this case than you first thought.

Denise tells you that Jason fluctuates emotionally (the same as any other autistic person). The only time he is truly happy is when he is being dealt with by the police. She realises this is not a good thing, but having sought help on many occasions, she has got nowhere. Switching to your autism awareness mode, you ask, 'How long has this been going on?'

'Ever since he was little. He is completely obsessed with you lot, sorry, the police an' that.' You could interview Jason at home and process the crime as usual, but you feel that something must be done to stem the offending pattern. Now you are starting to understand that there are other issues behind the repetitive behaviour and there really must be some intervention. You can initiate this, but only from inside custody. You explain this to Denise and arrange to bring Jason in at a convenient time for all of you.

In the meantime, you go and speak to the custody sergeant who is not happy with having someone in their suite who could be dealt with by voluntary interview outside. You explain that by having Jason in custody for a short while, arranging for social services and health care to be involved, you could start an intervention process that would prevent Jason coming back in again. They finally agree in these circumstances.

After speaking with Denise, you arrange an interview room that is bland and ordinary. You wear just a plain white shirt, leaving all of the other equipment outside the room. This is all to keep stimulation to a bare minimum. Jason is booked in with the least fuss and then booked straight to interview, again keeping everything low-key. By his demeanour you can tell that this is not pleasing Jason. Once in the room you explain the interview, but quietly, and carry it out straight away.

By not stimulating the senses, usually you would be following the Golden Rules exactly; however with this approach you can be doing the opposite. Jason seeks the drama and excitement he sees whenever he is arrested. By not giving him what he desires, you could be pushing his anger button. Having discussed this with his mum, she is aware and fully on board to deal with any issues that might arise.

You ask Jason, if he went to the house around the corner.

He replies quietly, 'Yes.'

'Why?'

'To break the fence.'

'Why?'

There is no reply. Jason drops his head. You can see that he is reluctant to talk about it. You change tack: 'Do you like the police, Jason?' Immediately you see a spark of interest, he nods. You get him to affirm this in speech, then ask, 'Why?'

'I like your uniform and the radio and the cars, everything. I have a collection...' He continues to speak about his special interest. Once he has gone on for a short while, you interrupt him:

'Do you understand what we do, Jason?'

He looks quizzically at you and says, 'Yes,' as he does know.

'Do you know we stop bad people doing bad things and also help good people and save lives?'

'Yes.'

'When I'm in here talking to you, how many bad people am I going to catch?'

Jason thinks. 'None.' It is a logical conclusion.

'That's right, none...and how many people could I help or save their lives whilst I am in here talking to you?'

'None.' Again, logical.

'That's right. When I am in here talking to you, because of the thing you did I can't go out in my car and help people. That is a bad thing isn't it?'

'Yes,' Jason agrees, as it is.

'You see Jason, every time you damage something, a police person has to stop doing good things and locking away a bad person, who hurt people like you and your mum and you want me to lock them away, don't you, Jason?'

'Yes,' he replies quieter.

'Yes, because you have people who say bad things to you and your mum, don't you?'

He nods.

'When you are scared or your mum cries because of the things the bad people do, like throw stones at your windows, you want the police to catch them, don't you?'

'Yes.'

'Well I do too, but if we have to go and talk to the man whose fence you broke, I might not be able to come and help you, do you understand?'

Jason thinks and then replies, 'If I keep doing bad things, then you won't help my mum?'

'Hmm, not won't, Jason, but can't. I always want to help and I will if I am not busy dealing with all the stuff you have broken.'

'Okay,' he replies.

'Okay what, Jason?' you ask hesitantly.

'I won't break anything again, I don't want to see mum cry.'

Mum starts to fill up and places a hand on Jason's shoulder.

'That's good, Jason. I am going to end the interview now and I will leave you with your mum. I want to see if the lady I asked to come is here. Are you okay talking to a lady if mum is with you?'

'Yes.'

You leave the room, book Jason back in with the custody sergeant, then speak to the woman from social services you managed to persuade to come in. During this conversation, you update her that Jason seems to have turned a corner but will need a lot more support to continue and his mum really needs some help. She sits with both of them whilst you arrange bail and probably an out-of-custody disposal with the sergeant.

By doing this, you have intervened in a circle of criminality which has been going on since Jason was a small boy. The measures you have used reduced the stimulation for his obsession. Removing your uniform and utilities and making him come on the bus to the police station all added to the sense of disappointment. Usually by offending he received the 'buzz' he wanted; he got to meet the very people he adored. Showing Jason that police work is not all glamour, it has a mundane side and he will not get the ride in a police car or have handcuffs put on him, hopefully will demonstrate that he cannot use the police as his own toy.

DEBRIEF

Caution must always be used when dealing with anyone with an obsession, as the last thing we want is to shift this absent area onto something else that is equally disruptive or even dangerous. This is why the officer in the scenario was putting in measures to help both Jason and his mum. If local health services, mental health or social services can assist, then bring them on board. Their expertise may be exactly the support a family needs. Working with health and council services to change behaviour can be an excellent route if available.

If the services will not or cannot assist you, search wider afield. See if any of the local autism charities or the carers support groups can help. They can offer advice on a number of levels for families who are struggling and have possibly dealt with similar situations.

It may be that the family, like Denise, have not been successful with local services, so have given up and tried to manage everything themselves. Your sensitive contact could be just the catalyst they need to seek guidance or ask for help. Being isolated for as long as Denise has can leave them surrendering all hope. Speak to them and see what you can do. They may reject any offer but at least give it a go. You will lose nothing in trying.

The techniques used by the officer in the interview will help with any autistic person who can feel overwhelmed by a uniform or police apparel. If needs be, remove what you can or feel comfortable without. It can go a long way in reducing stress or, conversely, stimulation.

A police obsession is a difficult one to deal with but can be more common than you may imagine. Use the Golden Rules and THINK AUTISM if you are ever called to one and you may have a better outcome.

In your mind

When you are next driving to a job and hear the word autism, what will you be thinking? I hope you will now have an open mind. Try not to over think the job before you get there. Yes, you now have a wealth of knowledge gained from this book, but still do not assume anything. The people you will be dealing with are just like the rest of humanity and have all of the same foibles.

Be open, friendly and free-thinking. Take account of everything around you and in particular, what may not be being said. A lot of autistic people, their families and carers have a deep mistrust of the police. This could be just the opportunity for you to rectify that view.

Try not to have any preconceived ideas but be mercurial in your thoughts. Also, don't be afraid. As I have said many times already, autistic people are a lot more forgiving than most. Tell them how you are feeling, 'cough' to your fears or lack of knowledge. Mention this book if you want. Tell them that you have actually read about autism and are willing to learn more from the real experts: them. They may have a wry smile on their face, but don't assume this is sarcasm; they will have been told lots of times before by NTs that they know best.

Be prepared to make quick changes (we can't, but you can). If something doesn't go right, then change to something that will. For instance, if you go in all happy and smiley but the person with autism is unresponsive to your effervescence then tone it down a bit but don't just give up. They are entitled to be reserved until they know you better. On the other hand if it is a more extroverted household then go with it and see where it leads.

Use time in the car (or on foot if you are lucky enough) before you get to the job to run through what this book lays out. Don't panic, don't worry and do engage.

The best piece of advice I can give you is:

If in doubt, *ask*.

Chapter 3

Autism in the Wider CJS

Dealing with victims and witnesses

When dealing with a person with autism, use the advice contained in this book, as it has been designed to assist you at whatever stage you are in the CJS. The watch words for working with autism are: patience, sensitivity and understanding.

These apply to investigation with an injured party or witness with autism. Treat them carefully and you will obtain your evidence. It may take a little longer than with the people you usually encounter but the information will be there, just not in the way you may have thought. Above all, please reassure them that you *believe* them. Many autistic people will not report crime in the first place as they fear they will not be believed; keep assuring them this not the case.

Be vigilant for any signs that they are being harassed, pressured or threatened to withdraw their complaint. Autistic people can be very vulnerable to outside influences, so do your best to safeguard them throughout the whole procedure.

If the statement can be done in their own home, this would be the best option. If you feel that the home environment is not conducive to that end (for whatever reason), then think about showing the person the location prior to the statement being obtained, even a day or more in advance. If the person with autism has come in, has seen the location and has been able to leave without any stress then it could prove a positive enough experience for them to come with even less stress next time. I am conscious that this must be balanced with a false expectation of leaving the next time without having to give the statement. The carer/AA will be best placed to advise on the suitability of each route.

The way in which you obtain a statement will have to be adapted to suit the person with autism and all of the considerations I have already suggested must be used in order to protect them from the ordeal of the process.

An autistic person may have locked the incident down and be unwilling to release it. This is a completely natural reaction that many people who have suffered traumatic events encounter. The mind's incredible ability to protect us is still being studied. With autism this can be amplified as the person may not have the cognitive ability to express all of their feelings, which I have explained previously.

As with any victim it can be a terrifying experience talking to the police; however, this can be even more traumatic for an autistic person where their emotions, fear, anxiety and stress could be magnified due to the extreme nature of the situation.

An autistic person can feel as if they are back in the exact moment the incident happened, emotionally as well as mentally. It may be just as distressing and disturbing for them, no matter how many times they revisit it. The emotions may never go away; the pain and fear will be exactly the same. Speak to their carers and health professionals about support for them after you have obtained what you need.

The officer may see the victim/witness flinch every time they reach the same place, as they are seeing it in their mind as if they are back there. Try to work around that, rephrasing the question or skipping ahead to save the witness from reliving this particular part of the incident. The carer/AA may help with making suggestions specific to the person they care for.

If video-witness recording is being used – something that can prove extremely useful for autistic people – then take the time to fully explain every part of it. Just loading it up and saying, 'Right, tell me what happened' can be a very stressful experience. Ease the person in slowly, allowing them to become comfortable before commencing. The autistic person may assume they are on TV and be worried it will be shown to all of their friends, embarrassing them. Ask them how they feel about it and once completed, debrief them fully, telling them they have done really well. Also tell them what happens to the recording next and how it is an integral part of the investigation process, just as they are too. A little praise goes a long way with autistic people.

Use the same approach as with the custody section to question and obtain evidence. Do not assume the autistic person can sit for long periods without becoming distressed; speak openly to them and their carers about refreshment breaks, even in their own homes.

Assure the autistic person you believe them. A lot of vulnerable people have been made to feel their opinions and thoughts do not matter. You are an important person in their eyes and whatever you say will be believed unquestioningly. They will respect you and act upon your suggestions. This can be used to support or destroy their confidence, from one misplaced word or throwaway comment. This is why you must be careful in how you deal with them.

Do not tell them you will find the offender or they will go to prison when there is absolutely no chance of this. Like all witnesses, treat them with respect but be careful not to get their hopes up when you know the opposite is true. Be honest with them but not brutal.

As you are writing things down or making notes during the recording, stop and tell them it is positive thing, as they may think you are writing something bad about them. Reassure them you are there to support and assist them.

When searching for information, going through the incident once before you actually record it could be assumed by the autistic person to have accomplished the task. If you are going through a cognitive interview programme or you wish to jump ahead to an exact point then explain this. Tell them you will return to the start when this section is complete.

Alternatively, if you wish to use their own logical approach and plough through the incident from start to finish in one go, then explore this area. It could be that even though they give you far too much detail you will get everything you want and so will they.

A reluctant injured party (IP)/witness is always frustrating. Talk to them openly; ask them why they don't want to engage with you and also their carers. Use the rules and advice in this book to reason why. Could it be you that is making them uncomfortable? Do not be angry about this; they have the right to feel how they do. It may just take a tiny adjustment and they will engage with you. Use my anxiety/stress section to understand what is going on in their mind. It is *your* responsibility to put them at ease, not theirs to adjust to what suits you.

Mate crime

There has been a lot of work done across the country with autistic people, concerning 'mate crime'. I personally worked with charities and councils trying to protect vulnerable people from this abhorrent abuse.

Due to their sometimes isolated living and desire to 'fit in', autistic people can present an irresistible target to people who can see them as a source of a steady stream of cash or a place to stay and therefore exploit them. The victims rarely report the crimes for fear of the perpetrators or shame. This makes the efforts of the organisations who are working to tackle this even more important.

If you are called to a report of a disturbance, vigilance is paramount. The occupier may be surrounded by unusually younger or older people than you would associate them with. This can indicate they are being targeted by specific groups for a reason. Look for signs of autism listed in earlier sections.

STOP. THINK. Is this person autistic?

If you are suspicious of the crowd around the person, disperse them. The person is much more likely to talk to you if alone and feeling safe. Reassure them that they can talk to you openly and honestly. Tell them you are there to help. If you can contact their carer, do so. They too may have suspicions but have previously been unable to voice them. Look for signs of abuse, for instance marks on them or their home in disarray. Anything that can be done to stop these crimes should be done.

Mate crime can start with just one person pretending to be their friend. Starting with getting to know them and being nice, quickly it will turn into pressure to loan money or stay the night. The cash never gets returned and the person may never leave. Abuse can easily occur, mental as well as physical. Signs that this is happening may come from the carer who will say that the autistic person always wears long sleeves now or has stopped visiting them. This isolation only adds fuel to the offender's crime.

The autistic person may not be aware that the crime is actually occurring. Having not had a previous friendship or relationship, they may assume that this is how they work. The offender may be telling them the same thing. Unpicking the details behind something that you have been called to is going to be tricky, but it is vitally important that the case is properly investigated, if the autistic person is to be protected.

You might be called by a carer or other support staff who have seen something that worries them. Listen to their concerns and act upon them, even if it is just to speak to the alleged victim.

If you can take the autistic person to their carer or a day centre where they are known, then do so. Get them to a place of safety before questioning them further, away from the damaging environment, where the truth could be more easily obtained.

Watch what they say and how they say it. If they deny everything or insist all is fine, probe a little deeper and ask around the people who know them. They may be refusing to engage because the offender or one of their friends is close by.

Again, think of where you are and how you are presenting to the person with autism. Give them time to process what you are saying and if it seems lost on them, try a different technique. Use the advice in this book to achieve the best for them.

Do not assume that mate crime is something that is confined to autistic people and the offender being NT. It is an offence that can easily be committed between autistic people. The injured party may not want to report the crime as they feel that 'telling on' a person like them is wrong. The autistic community is quite tightly knit and breaking down the abuse from within it could take some investigating. Following the Golden Rules and using the section on autistic offenders will assist you here.

Once a crime has been identified, set up a line of contact for the person as they are the one who is going to have to go home and face the problems left behind. If sheltered accommodation is suitable and available then this may prove a useful tool in rebuilding their confidence. Seek help from all those around the person with autism as they will be best placed to assist. Above all LOOK, LISTEN and THINK when dealing with autistic people and mate crime.

Post investigation

It is always a sound strategy to place the victim at the heart of any investigation, as so much attention can be diverted to locating and processing the perpetrator. Regular updates to the victim and their AA are just common courtesy but will mean so much to the autistic person. Families are often overlooked or disregarded by many services, so it is vitally important to stay in contact to prevent any withdrawal of the complaint.

I fully recognise the constraints of an investigation and all that goes with it but I cannot overemphasise the importance of keeping an autistic IP 'in the loop'. This could be the only thing they are thinking about 24 hours a day.

It doesn't have to be a visit (although why not?); just a phone call is enough to show you still care about their case. Do not say you will come round and see them once a week when you have no intention of doing that. If you know you are going on leave for two weeks and then on a course which will mean you won't be able to contact them, then tell them. If you hide the truth, when it comes out that will destroy any faith they have in you.

If you think ahead and ask a colleague to check in, run this by the IP/witness too. Having someone they are not expecting can cause them a great deal of stress. Again a simple phone call could be all it takes, but visits are usually better, unless they or their carer have asked for calls or even no updates at all; work with what they actually want. They may not want to be reminded of it all until they have to attend court or the case is over.

If a witness referral service is available and it is possible for it to also link in with the person, all the better. In the rare circumstance that you have an RI then use their expertise fully to form a circle of trust with the victim as soon as possible.

In the custody section, I stated that telling an autistic person you will do something and then not doing it is counterproductive. It was the example of the counting detainee I used: 'I'll be back in five minutes'.

Remember, when dealing with an autistic person, always use this maxim: If you say it, then mean it.

The autistic offender

An area of the CJS often forgotten or overlooked is the alleged offender. An autistic person like Daniel in Example 9 can find themselves in trouble because they have done something that is a logical conclusion to the situation.

An autistic person may have a nasty neighbour who they receive abuse from on a daily basis. In their mind, throwing a brick at the nasty person when they shake their fist once again could be the final straw after suffering years of abuse from them.

There is no conscious malice intended. All they want to do is stop the neighbour from being nasty to them and their family. The intention to harm the person is completely absent. In that moment the autistic person will be scared, angry or upset and nothing more. Throwing the brick is simply something they have in their hand and what happens to the person it reaches will not have entered their mind.

The fact that the fist shaker was standing in their front room and the brick went straight through the window, shattering the glass and causing injury to them, was not considered at any point. Most of the criminal aspects of an offence will usually be missing and what you will be left with is a rather simple explanation.

This scenario can be transposed to many different situations across the land in countless ways and with countless results. The actions will be different but the mindset will be exactly the same: I did this because they did that. It will be how they perceive the trigger that has caused them to carry out the act. This is not an excuse, it is just an explanation.

Putting a habitual offender to one side for the moment, it is the first time defendant I wish to discuss. These are the 'unfortunately not so rare' navigators of the CJS. Circumstances, like those above, have dictated that the person with autism is now attending court as a defendant.

The chances of having an RI from the very small group available are remote, so I will not include them here. The autistic person is left attending court at best with their carer or at the very least an AA. Assuming they arrive on the correct day at the right time, what awaits them is a frightening, confusing and archaic court system, too busy to be concerned about an autistic individual.

Up until the point where they walk through the court doors, the chances of any assistance will have been scant or down to the carer to arrange via a charitable organisation. The presumption of guilt seems to hang over those who have been charged and placed before the courts.

If they are found not guilty or discharged from court, they will have to rebuild what is left of their lives as best they can. The fact they have been freed from the process would seem recompense in itself; however, the mental scarring from having been placed in the system may never heal. The person with autism may always feel tainted by the ordeal, becoming insular, perhaps refusing to leave the house in case the situation happens again, even though it was through no fault of their own.

If a guilty sentence is passed then they should be asked to engage with the National Probation Service (NPS) to produce a pre-sentencing report. The following has been obtained from the Crown Prosecution Service website,[1] section pre-sentence reports:

The purpose of a pre-sentence report (PSR), as defined by s158 of the Criminal Justice Act 2003, is to assist the court 'in determining the most suitable method of dealing with an offender'.

The report should include:

- an analysis of the offence and pattern of offending, beyond a restating of the facts of the case

- relevant offender circumstances with links to offending behaviour highlighted; relevant circumstances may, for example, be related to an offender's mental health or disability

- the outcome of pre-sentence checks with other agencies

- sentence proposals that address the offenders assessed risk and needs, and

- for offenders aged 18–24, a consideration of their maturity must be included.

---

1   www.cps.gov.uk

The person's autism should have a bearing on the outcome of the case. Their cognitive ability or comprehension of the offence should be investigated by the NPS. This is, unfortunately, one more ordeal the person with autism must endure in order to receive a fair hearing.

If anything can be done to prevent this from happening at the point of arrest onwards, then I urge you to think about it very carefully. Charging and bailing may be the end of your involvement with the offence, but to someone with autism it is the start of a very long road of anxiety.

Consider this: 'Is this really the right outcome?'

This leads straight back to the section above and it should now be clear as to why I have tried to weave a line of thought throughout the whole CJS process. Your decision on how to deal with a person with autism has a huge impact on their lives and you could be responsible for intervening in a circle of offending or even diverting them from the whole CJS; you have that much power.

Please use it wisely.

In the next example a young autistic man is a repeat offender who finds himself being arrested once again.

EXAMPLE 10

Robert has been living alone since he was 17 years old, when he was kicked out of his family home due to his violent episodes. The local authority has a series of bed-sits turned over to young people to enable them to learn to live independently. A social worker visits them on an ad-hoc basis to check they are coping and abiding by any orders in place by the courts.

Now 21, Robert is out of work due to his unstable demeanour and unreliability. He exists on the meagre benefits he receives and anything he can lay his hands on to sell.

From a young age, Robert did not attend school as he was told he couldn't learn and didn't fit in. It was from here that his anger issues arose. Feeling worthless and having few positive role models, he descended into alcohol and drug abuse. After some success with a rehabilitation scheme from a young offenders institution, he managed to kick the Class A drug habit but moved more heavily into alcohol abuse.

Whilst in prison Robert was diagnosed with autism. He still doesn't fully understand what it means but feels it is a negative label. He has not received any intervention or education surrounding his tri-fold diagnosis (Asperger's, ADHD and OCD).

Yesterday, Robert was offered a cut of the money from a burglary, should he be willing to scale the drainpipe and open the skylight. He agreed as he is still agile enough to do things like this with ease. After the offence was carried out, he was given his share of the proceeds and immediately went to the local store and purchased some strong, cheap cider. He then wandered off to the graveyard and consumed it all over several hours.

Robert feels comfortable in the graveyard but it always makes him melancholic. His grandparents are buried there side by side and visiting them reminds him of the only time in his life he was happy: in their company.

He manages to stand and makes his way to the gate where an officer is walking past. He sees Robert first and knows him extremely well, having arrested him several times for the same thing: drunk and disorderly behaviour.

Robert swings his bleary head towards the officer; he sneers at them and comes out with what will inevitably get him arrested. The stream of expletives aimed at the officer cannot be ignored in this usually peaceful neighbourhood.

The officer requests assistance as Robert is a handful and not to be tackled solo. He is warned many times to go home but refuses and ends up fighting with the officers. He is detained and delivered to custody. Once there he is bundled into a drunk cell (one with a lower bedding platform) and left to sober up with regular checks to his cell.

Upon presentation to the morning sergeant, Robert has calmed down and is nursing yet another hangover. The sergeant has no option but to charge Robert and bail him to the next available court. Robert simply shrugs; he has seen it all too many times to care.

Before he is dealt with, the sergeant looks into his previous records and sees that he has refused to link in with the drug and alcohol intervention agency on each of his custodial stays. The custody officer asks him to see them now as they are in the building and willing to help. Robert refuses. Undeterred, the sergeant explains that in his opinion, Robert is still intoxicated and therefore unable to make a conscious decision. He is returned to his cell to sober up. This does not please Robert, who bangs on the door, demanding to be released.

What the sergeant has done is use the information on his system and the marker for autism to try to arrange a meeting with the dependency worker. Although he has been assessed previously by an HCP and not deemed in need of an AA, he is still vulnerable due to his autism.

Eventually Robert calms down and both the sergeant and worker visit him in his cell and talk his predicament out. He agrees to a private consultancy with the worker and after their chat, has a full appointment made.

Even though he is still charged and bailed, conditions can be placed on him to engage, albeit willingly this time, with an addiction programme. This he does and continues to do so well after his court case.

DEBRIEF

Robert was a successful case. Up until his autism was finally highlighted from his record, he had gone unassisted. The use of an AA was raised with a resident HCP who said quite bluntly there was nothing wrong with him. Apparently his Asperger's, ADHD and OCD weren't enough to warrant him one. This was eventually challenged and a reappraisal was agreed if he came in again; thankfully he didn't.

Robert kicked off big style when returned to his cell. He shouted all the names under the sun but after he was repeatedly offered a solution, he eventually calmed down enough to engage with the custody team. The drugs worker was excellent and did all of the hard work in gaining his trust.

The bail conditions were justified to place a legal obligation on him. He was a bright lad and someone who had never been given a chance to show it. By intervening, it gave him the opportunity to stand back and reassess his life. The courts thought the same way and he was given a rehabilitation order. Thankfully the drugs worker managed to change his offending behaviour and although he did fall off the wagon a few times, he didn't come back into custody. It was reported that he even managed to find a job.

This is how you can make a difference. It can happen. With the right intervention and hard work, miracles can occur. The person you are dealing with needs to be on board. If they are not, then your job is all uphill. I've met hundreds of them, and a whole host of Robertas too.

STOP. THINK. Are they autistic and can you help them?

Remember, the work done with addiction during their involvement in CJS should be tailored to their autism. There are many charitable organisations involved in autism-specific help who may be able to assist them. If you cannot find one locally to you, link in with any of the drug/alcohol agencies working with custody; although they may not have autism training, you now have all of the advice in this book with which to assist them. The aim is to get the individual free of the addiction. The workers are skilled at doing that and the autism can be a side issue when dealing with some of the drugs used. Speak to the agencies and work out a plan that best suits the autistic person. It is all a 'suck it and see' scenario. Be patient and be prepared to get your hands dirty, as it isn't always pleasant work.

The court process

Having to attend court is probably going to be the most stressful incident in an autistic person's life. They have already been through an awful lot just getting to this stage. The thought of now having to stand up and speak in front of lots of people will be terrifying.

Cast your mind back to when you stepped into the witness box, the very first time you gave evidence. Your stomach was churning, legs turning to jelly. The more often it is done the easier it gets but it still isn't a pleasant experience for you, the professional witness. So, treat the autistic person carefully and give them as much support as possible.

As their specific point of contact (SPOC), organise the most suitable environment for an autistic victim/witness when the time comes to a court case. Discuss it at length, telling them everything they need to know about the court building, what entrance they will be using, where they will be sitting and the inside of the court itself.

If an RI can be secured then use their expertise for dealing with vulnerable witnesses. Talk the autistic person through the evidence process and arrange a visit to stand in the witness box prior to the trial (how long prior to the trial can best be advised by the carer/AA). See if there are special rooms put aside for vulnerable witnesses or any measures the court will allow to ease their anxiety, such as only coming in on the day they are required or to be a phone call away with a large time frame to attend. The more that can be done to alleviate the stress the better.

Special measures can be authorised by the judge in charge of a trial; this can even in extreme cases be extended to the defendant. They are a series of adjustments, designed to make the vulnerable person feel more at ease in the oppressive court environment.

The following is from the Crown Prosecution Service website:

The special measures available to vulnerable and intimidated witnesses, with the agreement of the court, include:

- **screens** (available for vulnerable and intimidated witnesses): screens may be made available to shield the witness from the defendant, (s23 YJCEA – The Youth Justice and Criminal Evidence Act 1999);

- **live link** (available for vulnerable and intimidated witnesses): a live link enables the witness to give evidence during the trial from outside the court through a televised link to the courtroom. The witness may be accommodated either within the court building or in a suitable location outside the court, (s24 YJCEA);

- **evidence given in private** (available for some vulnerable and intimidated witnesses): exclusion from the court of members of the public and the press (except for one named person to represent the press) in cases involving sexual offences or intimidation by someone other than the accused, (s25 YJCEA);

- **removal of wigs and gowns by judges and barristers** (available for vulnerable and intimidated witnesses at the Crown Court), (s26 YJCEA);

- **video-recorded interview** (available for vulnerable and intimidated witnesses): a video recorded interview with a vulnerable or intimidated witness before the trial may be admitted by the court as the witness's evidence-in-chief – for adult complainants in sexual offence trials in the Crown Court. A video recorded interview will be automatically admissible, upon application, unless this would not be in the interests of justice or would not maximise the quality of the complainant's evidence, (s27 YJCEA). (Section 103 of the Coroners and Justice Act 2009 relaxes the restrictions on a witness giving additional evidence in chief after the witness's video-recorded interview has been admitted);

- **examination of the witness through an intermediary** (available for vulnerable witnesses): an intermediary may be appointed by the court to assist the witness to give their evidence at court. They can also provide communication assistance in the investigation stage – approval for admission of evidence so taken is then sought retrospectively. The intermediary is allowed to explain questions or answers so far as is necessary to enable them to be understood by the witness or the questioner but without changing the substance of the evidence, (s29 YJCEA);

- **aids to communication** (available for vulnerable witnesses): aids to communication may be permitted to enable a witness to give best evidence whether through a communicator or interpreter, or through a communication aid or technique, provided that the communication can be independently verified and understood by the court, (s30 YJCEA).

After their evidence has been given, carry out a full debrief (if possible) and keep the victim/witness up to date with any outcome. Their anxiety will be just as high after the event as before. Do not forget about them; they will be relying on you. Once the trial is over and your job as SPOC has ceased, tell them that the process has come to an end but refer them to any volunteer organisations that may help them if required. Conclude their ordeal and allow them to deal with things as they see fit. Work with the carer/AA to withdraw as sensitively as possible, as they may have become reliant upon your interaction.

Advice for the judiciary

Although once out of police hands only the investigating officer (IO) or witness liaison have any contact with the person with autism, this book is still valid for anyone involved in the running of the court system. The recent advent of RIs has taken some of the burden for witness care off the shoulders of court liaison services but as previously stated, their scarcity is still impacting heavily on the judiciary.

Special measures are only available for specific witnesses and in extreme cases defendants. However the funding and logistics can only stretch so far and in the remaining cases the person with autism is left to rely on the limited time of the IO or more likely their carers for support.

There appears to be a lack of understanding, perhaps through lack of training, around how stressful a court case can be for a person with autism. Time and again I have been told from those involved in the system, both witness and defendant, that they were simply sent the trial details and nothing more. I cannot understand in these enlightened days why a protocol has not been produced to deal effectively with these extremely vulnerable people with autism.

A first step would be to address training of the courts staff, covering the security on the front door to the clerks of the court. Separate training for advocates, however desirable, is unfortunately something which we can only implore they embrace. A large body such as the CPS can bring in this important education for their staff, but the vast array of defence representatives are employed by independent companies and beyond all but legislation.

This book can assist with a sound introduction into autism, how to spot it and deal with it, but I strongly suggest seeking quality training to embed the important issues that face all of those vulnerable people, especially autistic, in the CJS.

By law there are many measures which can be put in place for vulnerable people, but these are reserved for only the few who are deemed deserving. A far better system would be a more affable environment from the outset. Changes can be made to the court buildings that would benefit *everyone* who walked through the door and are just as likely to be nervous as someone who is vulnerable.

Consideration can be given to the lighting: harsh, glaring low-slung bulbs that fizz and crackle will feel as if they are piercing the skull of a person with autism. Exchanging them for low-energy LED devices will not only be cost efficient but will alleviate a major stress inducer.

Waiting rooms are notoriously stuffy in the warmer months and freezing in the colder ones. Again, an efficient heating system will not only be cost effective but will make everyone more comfortable. If the outlay is prohibitive, then allowing adequate ventilation could be a first step.

As with any system, those who enforce it are the most essential cogs in the engine. If staff are not on board, are not trained or fail to grasp the significance of autism, then the whole ethos collapses. Overseeing that the whole UK court staff are trained and are an informed team ready to engage with vulnerable people is an easy solution to a problem that has been highlighted in many reports over the last twenty years.

People with autism and all vulnerable members of society deserve to feel confident about their judiciary system, which at present is sadly not true. Reports from the autistic community give a grave overview that starts with fear of the police, through a lack of knowledge by court staff and ends with disappointment in the injustice of many cases involving autism.

To prevent a further decline in the mistreatment of people with autism, the CJS needs to be dramatically overhauled and an informed understanding of autism placed firmly at the centre. Research clearly shows a lack of sufficiently trained people throughout the CJS, which is only adding to the stereotypical perceptions being perpetuated about autism.

All the advice for the investigating officer in the sections above holds true for the Courts staff. Patience and understanding are just two of the essentials. Treating all autistic witnesses with respect should not have to be mentioned but sadly, it does. Talk to them as equals rather than subordinates and listen carefully to what they say. Their views are every bit as valid as the others in the CJS you meet on a daily basis. If you are unsure as to what they need or are requesting, then ask them clearly again. Do not assume you know what they want.

The research has been done, the conclusions have been made; now it is time to put the recommendations into practice and protect all vulnerable people who engage with the CJS. After all, isn't justice supposed to be at its centre?

Chapter 4

Autism in Other Areas

SPOC for autism

For best practice every force should have a specific point of contact for autism, someone who has training in it and essentially a passion for helping those with autism. Previously this post has not existed; only in the past few years has it come to the fore, now that awareness is beginning to filter through to the wider public services.

I have noticed that many of the SPOCs are officers with a diagnosis of autism. This is an excellent use of an advocate who is autistic and best placed to represent the rest of the force who may be autistic or neurodiverse as well as the wider community. Other officers who are too wary to admit they have or suspect they have autism may summon the courage to approach the SPOC and begin some kind of dialogue, which previously would not have been possible.

A force promoting the idea of autistic officers or a disability will be a huge boost for the local community, as it was with mine. The reception I received from the wider policing family as well as health organisations, charities and professionals was amazing. It can be only a positive step forward to show true diversity in acknowledging these officers.

A lot of anxiety in the autistic, indeed any vulnerable, community is that they would not be believed or understood. A SPOC who is one of them or at least highly trained and motivated will go a long way to allay those fears. However, to get an autistic SPOC, you will first have to find someone who is going to be willing to put their head above the parapet and say they are. This is an extremely tricky subject to discuss. It is akin to 'coming out' publicly and admitting you have autism. It is a much debated topic in forums around the world. Having done it myself, I can only explain how it felt for me and it may give an insight into the process.

After years of suspecting I thought differently to everyone else, I fought hard to even be seen by a psychologist, jumping through many hoops to finally meet with one. At the end of the process, I was given a diagnosis of Asperger's, dyspraxia, OCD and bizarrely, mild dyslexia.

Even though I now had the papers to prove my diagnoses, it took a while to comprehend. Eventually I realised I was still Andy, a husband, a dad, a police officer. It was just another part of me. I hadn't changed.

Having talked to others with autism (I thoroughly recommend it), this seems to be a similar pattern. The diagnosis you fight so hard to get suddenly becomes unimportant. The piece of paper it is written on isn't. That is so important when you start to fight the wider world (some agencies will not believe you even with it) but the words are not. The real point is knowing it yourself. That is what seems to matter most: clarification or even closure. Once (if) you have accepted it then possibly you can move on.

So, how do you tell people?

I was comfortable with who I was, so I did not find it a problem to tell everyone, but I had reached this stage by a long and fairly open route. For you it may not be quite so easy.

Do you tell your force?

That too is a hard decision. I was quite happy and secure in my job. I had served for twenty years, promoted to the rank of sergeant and was the force lead in my area. It may sound strange but I went straight to the top and told the chief constable first:

she had been my old sergeant and I trusted her. The two assistant chief constables were also friends who I had joined with, so I was very comfortable with them. They accepted it freely and as a result I became force lead for autism and the chairman for the Disability and Carers network, a support association within my force. This springboarded me around the country helping out charities and other agencies in autism.

My advice before you put pen to paper or 'come out' is to decide on the fallout on those around you. How will it affect them?

If you are in a relationship, does your partner know and how will they deal with it on a daily basis? Are you a parent? Your children may have to know. Your family you know best: will they be okay? Your mates, how will they take it? The people down the pub are bound to find out; will you be happy to walk into a bar where they all stare at you?

Finally, the force: are you quite sure you feel *completely* safe about telling them?

Talking to others in the job, there have been very different reactions around the country. The force cannot openly discriminate against you because that is against the law, but be very sure of your own circumstances before doing anything. Whatever you do, I wish you good luck and hope you receive the warmth, understanding and support you deserve. If you decide to keep it to yourself, please do not let it affect your mental health; seek professional help at every stage. There are numerous charities around the country working with the emergency services on just this subject, take a look at them too.

Community policing and engagement

I attended an autism outreach charity and spoke to the founder about police engagement. I was horrified when they said their members would rather keep silent about crime committed against them than report it to the police. When I asked why they simply explained that they were more scared of the police than of the offenders.

This worried me. After years of frontline policing, tackling crime and defending the right for people to go about their business unhindered, the thought of someone being frightened to report a serious crime was unthinkable. How had it arrived at this deplorable stage?

Further digging showed that the autistic people in that area had quite legitimately tried to report crime but were told there was nothing the police could do as they were not 'creditable witnesses'. This is totally unacceptable. However when I visited other charities across the country, I asked the same question and was given the same answer: 'We don't feel we will be believed.'

There seems to have been a wave of crimes committed against people with autism and very little done about it. The police may have attended many of these crimes but recorded a tiny percentage of them. When a search was done on the crime recording filters the word autism came back at an alarmingly low number. Whether that is due to a lack of putting the actual word autism in the correct boxes to return the crime or more likely the crimes having not been recorded in the first place, the percentage of vulnerable people reporting crime seemed incongruent with the amount I had been informed of.

Another concerning trend was the language officers used. In the main they seemed to have been 'polite' enough not to get complained about but came across as patronising, arrogant, aloof and condescending. Having witnessed this personally in custody with NT people then I can well believe the comments.

Autistic people are human beings, just the same as anyone else. They have feelings in the same way you do. They laugh, cry, worry and love exactly the same as *you*. They must be afforded the same courtesy and respect as you would like to receive.

People with autism stated engagement from local officers was woeful. There are a few in each divisional area and a handful across a police force who are doing wonderful jobs engaging and listening to the concerns of the vulnerable community. They show compassion and empathy with whomever they speak to. These officers' names were fed back to me time and time again. In my force and surrounding area, I made a point of visiting them to see why they were so good.

In the main there seemed to be a common thread: they had a child or other family member with a neurodiversity. They simply understood what it was like to suffer the strains of caring for them and sought out others in their community to try and reassure them they were there to help. However a couple I spoke to had absolutely no previous experience at all. So I asked them why they were suddenly so interested in the autistic community. They replied that they were just curious and wanted to know more. Most important of all, they saw autistic people as no different from anyone else.

It amazed me how their wonderful insight into the world of autism had derived often by chance but they had seized that opportunity and run with it. They engaged directly with a person, a school or a group then latterly the whole community just from one encounter. How many of us would do that? I spoke to their supervision (an immediate boss) about them. They said, 'That's just them, that is, we're always getting letters of thanks from someone...a cat up a tree, old lady lost, a kid fallen off a bike, they're a good bobby, that's all.'

Yes, they were good bobbies, but more than that they actively engaged with the *whole* community, not just the vulnerable or elderly, *everyone*. That is what community policing should and must be. It is not a poster campaign or open day once a year to let the public come and press the sirens on a car then hand them a balloon. It is more than that. It is a visible presence, speaking to people and *listening* to them.

Here is an example of how it can so easily be achieved:

Jeanette was away from her vehicle for the first time in months and actually walking in the neighbourhood.

As she walked past what seemed like a school, she looked to her left through large wire fence and saw a child of about eight in a classroom window. The child waved at her, Jeanette stopped and waved back. The child beamed at her and waved frantically with both hands. Jeanette grinned at the child's enthusiasm and out of pure curiosity she decided to pop her head in and say hello.

After pressing the buzzer, she waited for the side gate to click open, surprised by the level of security for such a small place.

Looking slightly nervous, the receptionist slid a glass panel to one side, before enquiring, 'Is there anything wrong, officer?'

Jeanette shook her head, 'No, just a general enquiry, that's all. I haven't seen this school before and wondered what it was as the fencing and everything seems very secure.'

The receptionist visibly relaxed, 'We are a special school. We have children here with learning disabilities and autism, so we need to keep them all safe.' She smiled.

'Oh, right. You see, I got a big wave from a child through the window and wondered if I could just say hello, if it's okay?' Jeanette asked.

'I'm sure that'll be fine but one moment whilst I call the head.' The receptionist returned to her desk to make a phone call.

After a few moments a woman appeared and smiled broadly at Jeanette. 'Good morning, officer. I hear that one of our students has attracted your attention. Do you want to have a look around and see what we do?'

'If that's okay,' she replied.

'Of course, we would be delighted and the children will be thrilled to see a real police officer.' She led Jeanette around and introduced her to the several classes including the one with the child she had seen. All of the children greeted her with an abundance of enthusiasm. At the end of the tour Jeanette was shown back to the reception.

'Well, what did you think?' asked the head.

'To be honest I really didn't know what to think when I heard it was a special school. It's great in here and the kids were all amazing!' she grinned.

'Spread the word and tell any of your colleagues to pop in and see us whenever they like. We are all inclusive here!'

Jeanette thanked her again and left feeling elated with the interaction. Over the next few weeks she went back several times and got to know a few of the kids by name, even seeing them when she went shopping off duty.

Through that one chance wave with a child her whole outlook changed when dealing with autism. She even went on to expand her horizons by visiting other centres on her patch and interacting with all sorts of people, cultures and carers. So did some of her shift.

Is this fairyland? No. This can happen and does happen, if an officer wants it to happen. Remember those 'good bobbies'? They were all beat officers and had a tray full of crime complaints to work through. They responded to all of the immediate responses they were given, but they all still found time to *stop* and *engage*. Were they superhuman? No. They just cared enough to spend 10 minutes out of a busy week to put a genuine smile on an autistic child's face.

All minority communities will say the same thing: there is not enough real engagement with them. Putting a member of their community on a board to tick a box is not community policing. I appreciate fully the constraints of budgeting, the ever-increasing demand on officers, cuts in numbers and all that goes with it, but if officers are universally directed from the top (not encouraged, but told) to engage with the communities around them as they go about their duties and allowed time to do it, then you would see a marked increase in detections, intelligence received and most of all positive feedback.

Fear of engaging with a minority community is understandable: fearing looking stupid because you don't know the language or how to address members of the community or what the protocols are is a completely acceptable emotion. However, it isn't rocket science. Speak to the support associations in your force to gain confidence at first or better still just go and do it. Knock on the door or the school, centre, mosque, whatever you would like to do. You will be surprised at how you are received. If it is with suspicion, then understand their concerns. You could be direct and try a bit of autism by being honest. Please do try it.

If your supervision (or you are the supervision) are reluctant to allow you (them) time to do this, then try a different route. Go down the performance development review (PDR) avenue. PDR or its newest replacement (it was just a yearly 'chat' when I joined) does have a place. There are plenty of sections for personal development; why not choose one of these to explore the local community and engage? There are plenty of ways to do it; the simplest is just go out and get on with it.

What is more useful? Sitting at the side of the road to do pocket books, in a vain hope of reassuring two elderly cats sat on a wall nearby, or going to a local community centre and talking to the regulars for half an hour?

I know what I have been told by many vulnerable people… and it is not the first option.

To sum up, there are many 'good people' in every force, doing excellent work and receiving very little recognition for it (setting aside the people they meet, that is). It is time you looked to these wonderful people, make them champions and learn from them just why it is they engage.

I feel that I cannot finish this book without showing you one example of how it can go right, from the start. This time, the Golden Rules have been placed firmly on top, in front and foremost.

Have a look at it and try not to think that it is cloud-cuckooland; it is again taken from a real-life experience.

THE FINAL EXAMPLE

It is early evening when PC Bloggs is called to a report of a suspicious person trying windows at the local high school. Upon arrival they check the perimeter but find nothing. They hear a sound of scuffling from the other side of a wall.

Jumping up onto it, they can see a garden area leading around a corner to the left. The noise is louder here, so they climb down and follow it. When they walk past the end of the building they can now clearly see a hooded figure sitting on the floor in the corner. The figure has their legs pulled up to their chest and arms wrapped around them.

PC Bloggs approaches them and sees that they are of slight build. The officer makes no attempt to hide their presence but is surprised to receive no reaction.

They stop about six feet away and call out to the person, 'Police, what are you doing here?'

They receive no reply but the figure seems to try to make themselves smaller. Their hood is tightly down over their face.

'Can you hear me? I am a police officer, you are on school premises, what are you doing here?' They call into control and update them: 'I have found someone just inside the garden bit, I'll update you further in a minute.'

The figure gives a muffled response, 'I'm just a someone and I know what you are, so go away.'

From the sound of the voice, the officer surmises they are a youngster. The response is unusual and not particularly aggressive. They try a different tact, 'What's your name then?'

'What do you want to know for? You're all the same, you don't care.'

PC Bloggs replies, 'Try me, you never know.'

The figure cocks their head towards them and pushes back the hood slightly, 'Why should I?'

PC Bloggs can see their hands are empty, so squats down but still keeps a reaction gap. 'You are on a school premises after hours and that is enough to cause me some concern. I would like to know who I am talking to, that's all.'

The hood is pushed all the way back, revealing a girl of about 16 years. She looks over at the officer. 'Who are you?'

'I am PC Bloggs. Who are you?'

There is a pause, then the girl says, 'I am Becky.'

PC Bloggs smiles at her. 'Well, Becky, now we know each other, what are you doing here?'

Becky shrugs and looks away but does not reply.

There is something that is puzzling the officer. Why is she not trying to escape? She seems very sad and does not want to engage. From their recent autism training, PC Bloggs remembers that vulnerable people sometimes want to engage but may not feel they can. The officer tries one of the pieces of advice they learned:

'Becky, what are you doing here, eh?' they say softly.

Becky sniffs and wipes her eyes with her sleeve. 'They won't let me back in, they say I can't be trusted.' It is now obvious that she has been crying since their conversation began.

'Who won't, Becky?' they ask softly again.

'The school, they say I can't come back, but I don't know what else to do!' Becky starts to cry again.

'Right. So the school have excluded you?'

She nods. Wiping the tears away she continues, 'All I want to do is be in there and not get sent home.'

PC Bloggs gets a welfare call from control and quickly turns their radio down to respond, 'All okay here, just with a young lady, no problems, update asap.'

Becky sniffs and chuckles, 'I'm not a lady.'

PC Bloggs smiles. 'Well they don't know that do they? Becky, my legs are killing me, do you mind if I stand?'

'Do what you want,' she says and shrugs.

'Thank you.' PC Bloggs stands and stretches. 'Ooh, I'm getting old, Becky. Is there someone who is going to be missing you at home?'

She nods and lowers her head, 'Mum, but she will be proper mad if you turn up, she'll think I have been locked up again.'

'Well, you leave that to me, eh? Come on, Becky let's get you back home.' The officer indicates by pointing to the wall.

Becky stands and walks slowly in front of the officer. All the time she does this PC Bloggs is readying themselves for Becky to run off. This concerns them, but the compliance they seem to have developed is more important.

They both climb the wall; Becky is much quicker but actually waits for the officer. As they both approach the car, Becky turns to the officer: 'Can I go in the front please?'

The officer had intended to do this anyway but the request was unexpected. 'Yes you can, Becky but please do not touch any of the buttons.'

'I won't, you're okay you are, you know that?' she replies as she opens the door.

The officer smiles at the sudden change in her demeanour. Before they leave, PC Bloggs obtains her home address, full name and date of birth. A check reveals Becky has been in trouble numerous times for unruly behaviour as well as damage offences. On the system was a marker for escaping, violence and ADHD.

On the way to her home, Becky does not say a lot but smiles thinly whilst she taps her legs constantly with both hands.

Once they arrive at her home, Becky sits back in her seat and says, turning the opposite way, 'Mum doesn't understand me. She's going to shout at me. I don't want to go in.'

PC Bloggs knows that Becky cannot stay in the car. 'I will speak first and tell her you are not in trouble, if that helps?'

Becky mulls this over then replies, 'Okay, but I know she will shout at me.'

On the doorstep the officer stands in front of Becky, shielding her. They ring the door bell and Becky's mum comes to the door,

'What the hell has she done now?' she yells.

PC Bloggs knows that parenting can be difficult as they have two children of their own, but this is quite an aggressive response. The officer puts up their hands palm out to show they mean no threat then answers firmly but quietly, 'Becky isn't in trouble. Could I come in please and have a word...er' – they wait for her mother to answer.

Becky's mum seems flustered by this unusually calm approach. She replies slightly confused, 'It's Mary and...er yes, you can.'

'Thank you, Mary.' The officer turns to Becky, smiles and says, 'It is okay now'.

The conversation continues inside the house. PC Bloggs tells Mary that Becky was by the school but no offences have occurred. Mary explains Becky has recently obtained a diagnosis of Asperger's and it is still sinking in how it affects them all. She has previously been diagnosed with ADHD and struggles with the medication, not always taking it as prescribed.

The officer asks if there has been any support in place for Becky since she has been excluded. They are told there is nothing being done. It transpires that Becky is very good at woodwork but isn't allowed to do it because the staff are worried about her being so close to potential weapons due to her unruly behaviour.

'Have you heard of the new engineer's shed on the industrial estate?' PC Bloggs asks.

'No' they both reply.

The officer explains that it is a free enterprise that is charity run and is specifically for young people to re-engage with schooling and preparing for life. Both of them agree to visit it and see what they think.

PC Bloggs asks Becky if she will stay away from the school until she is given permission to return. She agrees, now knowing she may harm her chances of being allowed back in if she is caught there. The officer also advises Mary to seek support from Becky's health professionals and some of the local autism/ADHD charities in the area, to help with the difficult day-to-day issues she has raised.

The officer leaves wishing them good luck. The officer updates control that all is in order and states that if anything does come in about the school that they have missed, they will deal with it personally.

DEBRIEF

This example contains all of the elements that this book advocates and I would wish for in an officer dealing with an autistic person. First the officer treated Becky as a human being; they were polite to her, even though she was a potential suspect. This case was simple but shows how easy it can be to switch from interrogator to public servant, which is what we all sign up for when joining any of the emergency services.

The main elements of the example you should have picked out are:

- The officer saw a figure sitting down and did not immediately go charging over.

- They used the Golden Rules: STOP. THINK. ASSESS.

- The figure was sitting and offering no violence.

- The officer spoke initially as they normally would; there is nothing wrong with that at this point.

- They received no reply but asked the question again, in the same way, and then got an answer.

- Once communication was established, they lowered the radio noise and their own voice.

- They went down to Becky's level and engaged with her when they could see her hands were free from weapons.

- It became immediately apparent that Becky was upset and needed help, not arresting.

- Throughout it all they used Becky's name, to reassure her she was a person.

- It became obvious that Becky was vulnerable. She needed to be taken back to her carer, in this case her mum, but she was afraid mum would shout. The officer reassured her again that they would help her (not solve everything).

- Becky could have run off at any point. She did not as she trusted PC Bloggs. That trust was earned. The officer knew this and as no offences had been committed, took that gamble, which paid off.

- All the way through, the officer was updating control and passing information. In turn they were receiving data they could use to help Becky. Both parts of the force system were working perfectly.

- Becky had been excluded from her school. That is a major thing for a school to do and it will not have done it lightly. Becky could not see why she was barred. Work needed to be done around this, but it was something for external agencies to do. PC Bloggs was already thinking about what they could do. This insight proved to be invaluable later. They were thinking about Becky and putting her at the heart of this scenario.

- Mum was understandably angry and anxious. The way she reacted had been predicted by Becky. However, the officer dealt with it calmly and carefully, using her name to reassure her everything was fine.

- By engaging with both people, the officer became able to assist them both. This is community policing at its best.

- The final part was protecting Becky and showing her and her mum that her talents could get her back into school or even into a work place if she is supported. It has been an all-round excellent job by the officer. As I have previously shown, it *can* be done, if you want it to.

PC Bloggs initially had no knowledge that the person involved in this was autistic. Furthermore, they probably were not even suspecting the person in front of them was vulnerable. However, because they had read this book or from the training they had received in autism, a vital piece of advice had sunk in:

The Golden Rules can work in *any* situation, including ADHD, not just autism.

The person the officer saw may have been a violent offender, breaking into the school to fund a habit. They initially approached Becky with the usual defence reserved for an unknown offender situation. Once they realised that the person was not offending or offering violence, they were able to reassess and deal with it calmly. They also treated them as a human being.

I bet the officer (and you) were surprised that the person on the floor was a girl. This is a less common scenario but still very possible. Do not assume anything with autism. Male or female, treat everyone the same and give them the respect you would want for yourself.

Without a full check of the school it is not known if there has been any damage done by Becky and the officer has had the serial linked, so they can deal with it if it does come in. This way they can assure continuity but it is unlikely that she has damaged anything, as the main aim was to enter an open window but this was not achieved.

Also keep your control updated but do not feel under pressure to give a full account. Likewise if you are in the control room, do not badger the officers for updates. I appreciate there are protocols and their safety is paramount but by coming across the airwaves three or four times in a short space of time, it can annoy the person the officer is dealing with. However if you do discover an important piece of information that will advise them on how to deal with the person and they are reluctant to talk to you, consider a personal message to tell them the person is autistic.

This is a delicate balance between satisfying everyone in the loop and doing the job effectively, but if you are all trained, it will flow so much better.

By dealing with Mary in the same way as a previous scenario, the officer calmed her initial anxiety and reassured Becky that they have kept their word. There is no guarantee this will work; many times I have failed to even get a full sentence out of my mouth when dealing with parents. The main aim is to engage with them and at least try. Keep calm in all situations and you may get the result you are aiming for.

Becky is possibly the more usual person you as an officer will come into contact with. They are quite capable of communication but will be reluctant to engage as they have met many police officers before who have not followed the Golden Rules and gone hands on straight away. Would you have bent down and simply picked Becky up by the arm because she failed to answer your questions?

I hope that your answer to that is no. I can tell you that had you grabbed Becky by the arm she would likely have swung round and punched you squarely in the face, as she cannot stand being touched. It is this very scenario that has resulted in numerous assault police charges and resist arrest which are on the system as markers. After all the advice you have now been given, spending a few minutes assessing the situation could give you the correct solution.

Please take these nuggets away from this final scenario:

- Follow the Golden Rules and the advice in this book.

- Do not go hands on unless you have to.

- Listen to what the autistic person is telling you.

- Be patient with them and their families.

- Treat *all* vulnerable people with the same respect you would want for yourself.

Do not be afraid to try all of these techniques and tweak them to your own ends. This book is just the start.

Conclusion

The CJS has been around since ancient times, not really being overhauled until the early Victorian era. The advent of the police to uniformly administer the law was one of the first visible indications to the public that 'justice' was being done.

The reform of prisons since then and the numerous amendments to the criminal laws have improved a person's chances when seeking justice. The introduction of several acts to tackle the disparity between NT and all disabled people has gone a long way to close that gap. However there is clear evidence that the injustice for autistic people is still a problem.

There needs to be a greater understanding of autistic people before the laws of the land are amended or new ones for them are created. Paying lip-service by agreeing that 'it simply isn't good enough, that; those type of people really do need help' doesn't really achieve a lot.

Many times I have seen comments designed to support autistic people failing to do that. To understand autistic people takes a desire or want to do so. Closed minds are the same as locked doors: difficult to get through. They must fully engage in the tuition or the process is pointless.

How is this achieved? By direct intervention through quality training and a greater visible presence from the autistic community. There are barriers on both sides and an intermediary system needs to be created to facilitate an exchange of ideas and views from all parties.

I have already mentioned 'quality training' but want to expand on it a little. The reason training can be far more effective when using people who are autistic is that they understand how autism affects them on a daily basis. By this I mean an autistic person can tell you how they feel in that particular situation or if you did 'that thing'. Answers will be immediate and not 'learned' as you cannot be taught how to 'think' autistic, it is just the way we are.

Training must be delivered sensitively and with meaning, so those attending can clearly see how their use of intervention techniques will stop the person with autism suffering at the officer's hands. It must not be an ad hoc presentation with mainly stereotypical, PowerPoint slides, delivered by someone who claims to know what autism is because they have done a course in it. These types of delivery are already out there and have done nothing so far to help autistic people. However they have enabled vast corporations to absolve themselves of responsibility because they have paid someone to sign a form saying they have trained their workforce in autism.

There are many high-profile advocates for autism now; even those who are autistic are managing to find a platform on which to speak. It is the beginning of a new wave of support for those with neurodiversity. More and more of the population are tuning into programmes that are based upon autism. This thirst for knowledge should be grasped by these advocates and fed the correct names, terms and best practices with which to help all autistic people.

This book was conceived with just this in mind: to deliver meaningful information to those in the CJS. Police officers are the very people those who are vulnerable want to turn to in times of trouble. You have the power to steer how that first contact is dealt with. Too often we see that these encounters have gone so very wrong. With the correct training and the Golden Rules from this book, *you* can make so many people's lives better.

Tiny adjustments to the way you approach a vulnerable person will achieve so much.

Police officers the world over are revered and lauded on a daily basis; quite rightly so. However, what makes the headlines? The one bad case, something which has gone horribly wrong. News agencies love these and will exploit, twist and highlight them as much as possible simply to sell their papers. Who can blame them? We have all picked one up to gawp at the latest impropriety by a celebrity. It is human nature to want to know more.

By doing something good, something right, it is not the headlines you want to grab but the thanks from that vulnerable person or their carer. The feeling that when you go to bed that night, you have done a good thing. There is nothing better than that: true knowledge that without you that person may have died or gone to prison. You stopped that happening, you intervened and did what was right, because you knew what to do and how to do it.

Wouldn't that be a wonderful scenario? All of the emergency services right across the world, all doing the same thing, saving lives and ensuring justice is done.

This is not Elysium; this can be achieved for not much money and all that needs to change is your perception of what autism really is.

Final words

I want to take the time to explain where this book has come from and why I decided to write a book on autism and the CJS.

During nearly thirty years in a job that I loved, I saw vulnerable people suffering injustice because of a law system that just didn't seem to understand them. The strange thing was, I did. I got why they thought the way they did, and their sometimes seemingly illogical explanations, which my colleagues dismissed, I wholeheartedly concurred with.

After the long journey to obtain a diagnosis, I went out and listened to those in the autism arena. I found that injustice was everywhere. Not just within the realm of CJS but in daily life. I wanted to help and found I could within my role in the police force. I joined several partnership boards and worked with neurodiverse charities across the UK to improve understanding of this complex subject matter.

Being autistic is a daily battle that only those who are autistic can truly appreciate. There are many, many wonderful NT people out there, doing fantastic work with all of those who are neurodiverse. However, you have to be it to know it. Simple as that.

Too many times I have been told (and I am not alone), that because I am 'very high-functioning' – *their words not mine* – I don't need help. This is utter tosh. If you are neurodiverse, you *are* and it doesn't go away or get better even with coping strategies. Sometimes I do need help just to carry out simple daily tasks. It all depends on how my brain is functioning at that particular moment and is usually down to the stress levels around me.

Above all, autistic people, neurodiverse people, are human beings but are sadly not always treated like that. There is a massive lack of understanding in the NT world about what we are, how we think and feel. Too often I have assimilated into NT society and have heard disgusting terminology about neurodiverse people, a lot of the time by those who are either working with or for autistic people.

As an officer I didn't always get it right but I always put my heart and soul into the job I was doing. Because of my autism, I saw things others didn't; patterns and detail screamed out at me. This all added to the role I carried out and made me more adept at some things than others.

In custody, I had detained people who wanted to fold their own clothes before they were put away and others who simply felt they could not trust a copper. I had to earn their trust.

Many of my colleagues thought I was mad, too soft or protective of them. In some ways I may have been, but I have the satisfaction that through my personal intervention I stopped a few of them from ever coming back through that door again.

All neurodiverse people are human beings; they think differently to an NT but they still do think and they feel and love like them too. Autism is just another way of saying 'the world looks like this to me'. That doesn't mean that it is wrong or funny, but is just different.

Please take from this book that it is there to help. It is not designed to trip anyone up or highlight a section of the CJS that is wrong. The book was written to show the easier route, the better route, the route that will protect the autistic person but also the officer. The last thing I want is for someone to get disciplined or dismissed because of something they did with a vulnerable person. The most selfish reason is that somewhere along the line, a vulnerable person will have to suffer to get that result, but in stepping back, thinking and just reassessing the situation in front of them, the officer could ultimately save that person's life.

Learn from the examples, please try the rules out and if there are any charities or autism clubs nearby, go along, in uniform or civvies, and say hello. Don't be afraid to go near the neurodiverse please; it is not a disease, you can't catch it but may get carried away with their fabulous zest and energy for life. After all, they are people just like you.

My thanks go to the people throughout my career who taught me right from wrong (even though I ignored it all), to the wonderful people in the autistic world for showing me what humility really looks like and to you the reader, for taking the time to look at this book and hopefully take away all the good from it.

Index

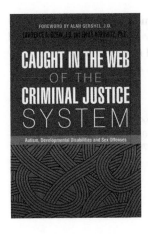

Caught in the Web of the Criminal Justice System: Autism, Developmental Disabilities, and Sex Offenses

Edited by Lawrence A. Dubin, J.D. and Emily Horowitz, PhD
Foreword by Alan Gershel, J.D.
Afterword by Tony Attwood

Paperback: £40.00 / $50.00
ISBN: 978 1 78592 713 3
eISBN: 978 1 78450 298 0
352 pages

Increasing numbers of people with autism and other developmental disabilities are being convicted of sex offences, resulting in draconian and public punishment. Yet even when evidence shows that people with these conditions often pose little threat to society, or lack a core understanding as to why their actions break the law, the "sex offender legal regime" doesn't allow any room to take the disability into account.

This ground-breaking book offers a multi-disciplinary examination of how unjust sex offense laws trap vulnerable groups such as those with developmental disabilities. Drawing on research, empirical evidence and including case studies, experts from the fields of law, ethics, psychology and sociology explore what steps should be taken in order to ensure that laws are just and take into consideration factors such as the vulnerability of the perpetrators. Investigating the consequences caused by public hysteria over sex offenses, this book highlights the judicial failure to protect defendants with developmental disabilities in the context of the unjust and hyper-punishment of all those charged with sex offenses. Proposing a new way forward based on research and evidence-based sentencing for sex offenses, and elimination of the sex offender registry, this book offers an informed and compassionate view that is essential for all professionals working in this field.

Lawrence A. Dubin is a law professor at the University of Detroit Mercy Law, specialising in legal ethics and litigation.

Dr Emily Horowitz is Professor of Sociology and Criminal Justice at St. Francis College in Brooklyn, NY.

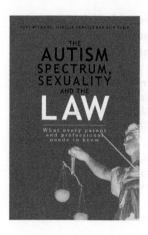

The Autism Spectrum, Sexuality and the Law What every parent and professional needs to know
Tony Attwood, Isabelle Hénault and Nick Dubin

Paperback: £14.99 / $19.95
ISBN: 978 1 84905 919 0
eISBN: 978 0 85700 679 0
224 pages

Based on Nick Dubin's own experience, and drawing on the extensive knowledge of Dr Tony Attwood and Dr Isabelle Hénault, this important book addresses the issues surrounding the autism spectrum, sexuality and the law.

The complex world of sex and appropriate sexual behaviour can be extremely challenging for people with autism spectrum disorder (ASD) and, without guidance, many find themselves in vulnerable situations. This book examines how the ASD profile typically affects sexuality and how sexual development differs between the general population and those with ASD. It explains the legalities of sexual behaviour, how laws differ from country to country, and the possibility for adjustment of existing laws as they are applied to the ASD population. With advice on how to help people with autism spectrum disorder gain a better understanding of sexuality and a comprehensive list of resources, the book highlights the need for a more informed societal approach to the psychosexual development of people with ASD.

A ground-breaking and honest account, this book will be an invaluable addition to the shelves of parents of children with ASD, mental health and legal professionals, teachers, carers and other professionals working with individuals on the spectrum.

Tony Attwood, PhD, is a clinical psychologist from Brisbane, Australia, with over 30 years of experience with individuals with autism spectrum disorders. He is currently Adjunct Professor at Griffith University in Queensland. He is the best-selling author of The Complete Guide to Asperger's Syndrome, Asperger's Syndrome: A Guide for Parents and Professionals, and the Exploring Feelings program manuals.

Isabelle Hénault has a master's degree in sexology and a doctorate of psychology from the Quebec University in Montreal. She has a private practice that provides assessment and therapy for individuals, couples and families, and acts as a consultant to a variety of organizations and schools. Her expertise lies in Asperger's Syndrome, with a special emphasis on sexuality, and she is the author of a sociosexual education programme for people with AS. She is involved with several international research projects on sexual education and psychotherapy for people on the autism spectrum.

Nick Dubin was diagnosed with Asperger Syndrome in 2004. Since 2004, he has been a leading advocate in the United States on Asperger related issues. He has a doctorate in psychology and a master's degree in learning disabilities. Dr. Dubin's hope is that his cautionary tale will open a discussion on AS and sexuality and prevent others with AS from ending up in the criminal justice system.

An Employer's Guide to Managing Professionals on the Autism Spectrum
Marcia Scheiner (Integrate Autism EmploymentAdvisors) with Joan Bogden
Illustrated by Meron Philo

Paperback: £16.99 / $24.95
ISBN: 978 1 78592 745 4
eISBN: 978 1 78450 513 4
256 pages

Employees with an Autism Spectrum Disorder (ASD) may be hugely beneficial to a workforce, but it can be difficult for individuals with no formal training to manage these employees successfully. This definitive guide will help managers and colleagues successfully interact with and support these professionals on the autism spectrum so as to ensure mutual success.

Integrate Autism Employment Advisors use their experience advising employers on how to successfully employ professionals on the autism spectrum to identify the everyday challenges faced by employees with ASD in the workplace and sets out reasonable, practical solutions for their managers and colleagues. Barriers to productivity are highlighted, such as the sensory environment, miscommunication, and inadequate training of colleagues. Easy-to-implement strategies to adapt the working environment are provided, such as agreeing on non-verbal cues to signal ending a conversation or establishing parameters for appropriate email length. This book is an essential resource for anyone who works with professionals on the autism spectrum. It will allow them to engage with and support their colleagues on the autism spectrum in a respectful way and help them achieve a greater level of working success.

Marcia Scheiner is President/Founder of Integrate Autism Employment Advisors. Previously, she had an extensive career in the financial services industry. She has a young adult son with Asperger's and lives in New York City.

Joan Bogden has been working in communications and training for over 30 years. She has an M.A. in Clinical Psychology from Fordham University, where she was a doctoral candidate and published researcher.